THE WORLD OF
COUNTRY
MUSIC

THE WORLD OF
COUNTRY
MUSIC

ANDREW VAUGHAN

FOREWORD BY
GEORGE STRAIT

LONGMEADOW
P R E S S

Thanks to Tony Byworth and Richard Wootton
for invaluable advice and assistance.

First published 1992 by Studio Editions Ltd.,
Princess House, 50 Eastcastle Street,
London W1N 7AP, England.

Copyright © this edition Studio Editions Ltd., 1992

This 1992 edition published by Longmeadow Press,
201 High Ridge Road, Stamford, CT 06904.

Design by Martin Lovelock

ISBN 0-681-41599-1

Printed in Singapore

0 9 8 7 6 5 4 3 2 1

Contents

Foreword

I am really proud to be a part of country music, not only because of country's amazing popularity right now, but also because of the back-to-basics sound that has proven to be a major reason for its success. I feel honoured to be a part of that success story and to be identified with traditional country, the kind of music I grew up with in Texas: western swing and the great Bob Wills and Ernest Tubb, along with my personal favourite, Merle Haggard.

Over the years, country music has been the subject of trends. We have seen it experience mass popular appeal only to fade away; but this time I believe it has really made its mark. The "New Traditionalists" of the 80s, such as The Judds, Ricky Skaggs, Reba McEntire, Randy Travis and myself, have helped put country music back on track. In turn, the doors were opened to an exciting new breed of young talents such as Garth Brooks, Clint Black, Alan Jackson and Travis Tritt. Multi-million selling records, top positions on the pop charts, an expanded video-market, prime-time network television programming and the tremendous success of country music's own networks have proven that country music is not just this year's fad.

Country's success is not restricted to the United States. Its popularity reaches around the world. When I made my international début in London in 1990, it was a memorable occasion made even more so thanks to a sold-out concert, to television and radio appearances and a genuine interest in country music among everyone I spoke to.

Country music has come a long way from the hills of the Appalachians and the Great Smokey Mountains, the farmlands and back-roads of the south and the great plains of Texas. Today, it is a phenomenal world-wide success story. Country music speaks a universal language. I am proud to be a part of that.

George Strait

Opposite, George Strait.
Strait's cool laid-back style
has seen him at the top of
his profession through the 80s
and into the 90s.

1
The Birth of Country

Country music came of age in America during the depression of the 1930s. This is when the Grand Ole Opry first took hold and when recording artists like Jimmie Rodgers, Bob Wills and Gene Autry became the first stars of country music. Even so, the music, in a variety of forms, had been around for much longer and musicologists have traced country tunes back to Elizabethan folk songs. This is not surprising, since it was the European settlers who brought their music with them and adapted it to their new lifestyles. As they faced incredible hardships and isolation, it is no wonder that country music developed a hard-hitting and melancholic edge. For example, while the words and tunes changed, the roots of the cowboy lament 'Bury Me Not On The Lone Prairie' are clearly traceable to the old sailors' tune 'Bury Me Not On The Deep Blue Sea', while the archetypal western tune 'Streets Of Laredo' originated as a British song about a dying soldier. Yet there

Left, Cowboy of the early 1900s. Note the rifle on the wall, the bottle on the shelf and fiddle in hand.

Previous page, top, Song sheet from 1915: cowboy laments and old folk songs whiled away lonely nights.

Previous page, centre, Music coloured the lives of poor southerners, as this Arthur Rothstein photograph from 1935 clearly shows.

is far more to the origins of country music than the gradual evolution of a European musical heritage, for the historical and geographical conditions of the South played a vital role in the development of country music.

European music was introduced throughout the United States but only really took hold in the southern states, where it continued to play a role many years later. As the United States blossomed into an enormously powerful industrial nation, the South was placed in a defensive position almost from the start. Electing for an agricultural rather than an industrial economy, it was to fight a long battle just to exist as the North marched confidently into the industrial age. The South, isolated, conservative and defeated in the Civil War, clung on to its heritage. The old songs became more significant and the hardships of poverty found a perfect release in a jaunty two-step or a sad ballad. The various regions of the southern states made use of local instrumentation, creating in a haphazard fashion what we know today as country music. Black music influenced rhythm, Mexicans in the West utilized the guitar, and everywhere the fiddle gave country its identifiably eerie and lonesome sound.

For years the music was all very down home and provided entertainment for rural communities, but the advent of new technology in the 1920s turned country music from a pastime into an industry. Radio spread the sound, helping to end the isolation of the South, and the new recording technology suddenly allowed musicians

Opposite, top, European settlers, c. 1900. The early pioneers had to be resolute in the new land. Their music was a simple form of entertainment which connected the travellers to their homelands.

Below, A farmer and his wife, barefoot and hungry, in Alabama in 1935. The 30s Depression caused massive social upheaval. The fact that country music spoke directly to the poor established it as the bedrock of American music. Photograph by Walker Evans.

Above and opposite, Western-style square dance from the 1890s. Jigs and reels from folk music were adapted to what rough and ready instruments the settlers could find. Country music could as equally soothe a sad soul as whip dancers into a frenzy.

Opposite, top, The Sons of the Pioneers, not only brought western songs to the movies and into the recording studios, but also launched the career of Roy Rogers.

and singers to pursue careers in music. By 1920 the record industry in America, while tiny in comparison with its billion dollar operations today, was in a healthy state. Major companies like Victor were reporting sales in excess of one hundred million records in 1921. Vaudeville tunes, band music and light pop classics were the order of the day. Nevertheless, it was a small company, Okeh, which was to introduce country, or hillbilly as it was then known, to the record-buying public.

A depression in 1921 severely hit the whole of the entertainment business. Radio, although in its infancy, was a real threat and Okeh had to find a new avenue for its operations. Instead of looking for mass appeal records, Okeh concentrated on specialist areas, initially with black or race recordings. Ralph Peer from Okeh chose to experiment with location recordings using portable equipment. In Atlanta, Georgia, Peer set about recording a pot-pourri of local musicians and singers. They all turned up – crooners, jazz bands, church singers, anyone with talent.

Eventually Peer was persuaded to record a hillbilly act, Fiddlin' John Carson. He cut two songs, 'The Old Log Cabin In The Lane' and 'The Old Hen Cracked And The Rooster's Going to Crow'. Peer was not impressed, describing the two songs as 'pluperfect awful', and failed even to give the recordings serial numbers. Even so, national sales of those recordings peaked at over half a million, showing there was a market and a great demand for hillbilly music.

In 1924 an opera singer named Vernon Dalhart, down on his luck, tried recording a hillbilly tune as a way of reviving a flagging career. 'The Prisoner's Song' became Victor's biggest-selling record in the pre-electric era, selling over six million copies. Other hillbilly singers got in on the act. Carson J. Robinson made quite an impact with story and topical songs, and Charlie Poole, Bradley Kincaid, the Skillet Lickers, Mainers' Mountaineers, Cliff Carlisle and Kelly Harrell carved out recording careers for themselves. Although these early artists found a measure of success, hillbilly or country music was still in its infancy. There were no stars to match those of band or popular light music, though the apparatus was in place to find them. Aside from the burgeoning record industry, radio was in boom and enormously significant in the spread of country and the nurturing of the first stars. In the pre-television age radio was king, with WSB in Atlanta playing hillbilly as early as 1922. The format was to be copied stateside with the radio show recording a live hoedown. The first major barn dance station was the National Barn Dance out of Chicago, which first went on the air in April 1924.

Hillbilly still needed some stars and it was Ralph Peer who discovered two of the biggest while on a reconnoitring trip in Bristol, Virginia, in 1927. They were the Carter Family and Jimmie Rodgers. Jimmie Rodgers was country music's first solo star and he is still regarded by many as the father of country music. His life story was as dramatic as the songs he wrote, and he died in a recording studio from tuberculosis at just thirty-three years of age. Rodgers started life on the railroads before being forced to quit because of bad health. In the mid 20s he worked as an entertainer in minstrel shows and won himself quite a reputation as a yodeller. Recorded by Peer in 1927, he won a contract with Victor and by the end of the year he was the company's biggest-selling artist. He drew heavily on the blues and his simple twelve-bar progressions, characterized by plaintive yodelling and heartbreaking lyrics, proved popular in the South and beyond. His influence on country, pop and, eventually, rock music cannot be over-

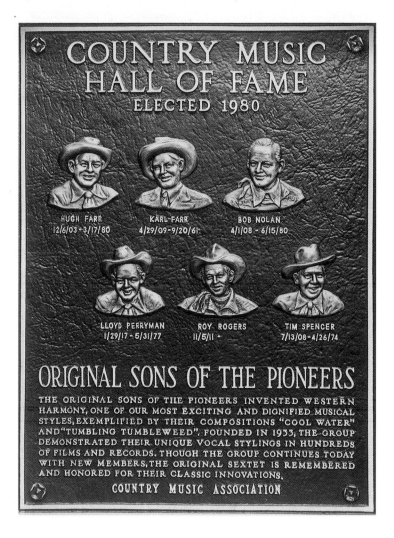

Left, The Carter Family: the original trio stayed together until 1943. A third generation Carter Family still performs today.

Above, The original Carter Family as displayed on a stained glass window in the home of Gladys Millard, eldest child of A.P. and Sara Carter.

emphasized. In his short six-year career he recorded over one hundred songs and sold over twenty million records. Songs like 'T For Texas' and 'Mule Skinner Blues' still surface in country artists' repertoires. Although Rodgers never played the Grand Ole Opry, his pioneering work was rewarded in 1961 when he was inducted as one of the initial members of the Country Music Hall Of Fame.

The Carter Family were also spotted by Peer on that trip. Indeed, Peer recorded both the Carter Family and Jimmie Rodgers on the same day, which must go down as the most significant single day in the history of country music. Part of the tradition of family entertainers, the group drew on old-time ballads as well as original compositions from leader A. P. Carter. With his wife Sara on autoharp and guitar and Sara's cousin Maybelle on vocals and distinct- ively finger-picked guitar, the family not only sold a vast amount of records throughout the depression of the 30s but also influenced those to follow and established a goldmine of songs that are regularly performed at old-time and bluegrass festivals around the world. The Carter Family has continued in various incarnations, with Johnny Cash's wife June Carter Cash continuing the tradition.

As the Great Depression set in throughout the 30s, country music was perfectly situated to respond. Radio was established, records were popular and star names had spread the word. Rural communities made the most of the emotional release of the music and danced their cares away to fiddle bands. With an industry in full swing, thousands of performers looked to country music to ply their trade and possibly follow Jimmie Rodgers to stardom and wealth. This dramatic interest in music led to the 30s being one of the most exciting and innovative periods in the history of country music. The basic styles were cross-fertilized, new genres like bluegrass emerged and a host of country artists appeared each year, many of whom were to have a lasting effect on the music.

Below, Jimmie Rodgers, The Singing Brakeman, was the first star of country music. A victim of tuberculosis, he died in a recording studio at the tragically early age of 33.

Right, Oklahoma migrants heading for the promised land of Oregon *c.* 1935.

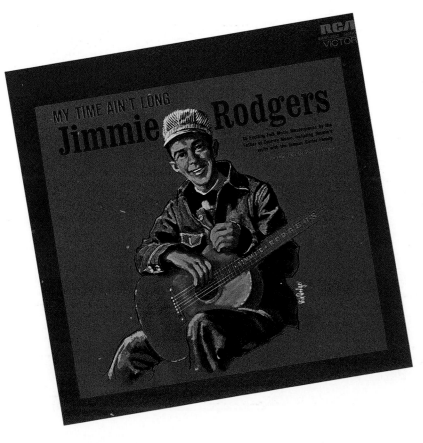

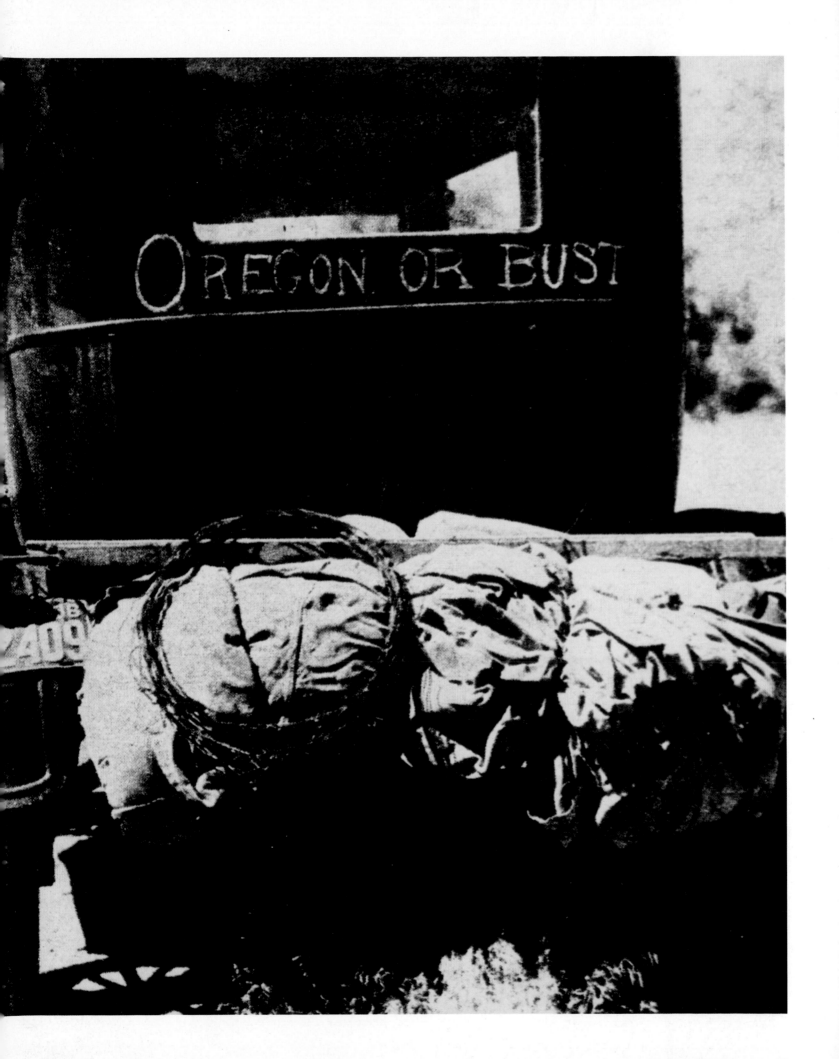

Of the radio stations involved at this time, it was WSM in Nashville with its Grand Ole Opry that became the most significant. The station had one of the most powerful transmitters in the South. The programme format came from George D. Hay, who introduced it as the WSM Barn Dance. Early performers included the Fruit Jar Drinkers, Dr Humphrey Bate and the show's first big star, Uncle Dave Macon. As the decades rolled on, the Opry would become the most significant vehicle for spreading country music around America.

Roy Acuff, a legend in his own lifetime as the first major star of the Opry and later co-founder of the powerful Acuff-Rose publishing company, emerged in the 30s. He set out to be an athlete but eventually settled for music and entertainment. He joined a travelling medicine show and in 1933 formed the Tennessee Crackerjacks. Acuff's style was cool, graceful mountain music. It was nostalgic, religious and perfectly suited America in the 30s. He made his recording début in 1936 with 'Great Speckled Bird' and 'Wabash Cannonball'. His repertoire on the Opry, which he joined in 1938, included such favourites as 'Wreck On The Highway', 'Fireball Mail', 'Night Train To Memphis' and 'The Precious Jewel'. A consummate entertainer, Acuff was the star of the Opry throughout the 40s, winning

Previous page, top, Very early picture of legendary country singer Roy Acuff, from the cover of a songbook. These publications still offer the public a popular way to learn their favourite songs.

Previous page, centre, Roy Acuff on the stage of the Grand Ole Opry at the Ryman Auditorium.

Right, Gene Autry, the most successful of all the Singing Cowboys, serenades Francis Grant in a scene from the 1936 movie *Oh Susanna*.

Opposite, Roy Rogers and his wife Dale Evans with Trigger. Rogers stepped into Gene Autry's boots while Autry served in the Air Force.

audiences with his easygoing showbiz manner. Aside from the heart-tugging music, he fooled around and even dazzled the crowds with yo-yo tricks. By 1943 he was earning 200,000 dollars a year. Acuff still performs on the Opry, his place secure as one of the founding fathers of modern country music.

While the string band sound (fiddles, guitar and bass) of traditional hillbilly mountain music continued through the 1930s, it was soon to evolve into a new sound. Two brothers from Kentucky, Bill and Charlie Monroe, changed the sound of string band music for ever, Bill Monroe eventually coming up with an original country genre, bluegrass. Bill, a mandolin player, brought energy and excitement to songs with a rapid finger technique. Where mandolin had formerly been a rhythm instrument, in Monroe's capable hands it was a driving force. This, together with high wailing vocals, was the basis for bluegrass. Bill and Charlie teamed up in 1935 and for three years the Monroe Brothers took duet acts to a new level of passion and excitement. They split in 1938, each forming

his own band. Bill Monroe and his Bluegrass Boys won a spot on the Opry, giving a wild version of the old standard 'Mule Skinner Blues'. This was bluegrass in its first incarnation, with guitar syncopated and driving, fiddle wild and fast, vocals high and screeching. But there was an element missing until Monroe came across, Earl Scruggs, a banjo player par excellence, in 1945. The music this band made from 1945 to 1948 is generally regarded as the standard by which all bluegrass music is judged. Monroe became a father figure for countless singers and instrumentalists over the years. The list of members of his Bluegrass Boys reads like a who's who of country instrumentalists – Scruggs and Lester Flatt (later to become stars in their own right), Don Reno, Red Smiley, Jimmy Martin and Carter Stanley (another bluegrass stalwart along with his brother Ralph).

In the 60s and 70s, rock bands and the country rock movement leaned on Monroe's pioneering work. The drive and passion of Monroe's style made bluegrass a close cousin of the rockabilly music that emerged in the 50s. It is

significant that his 'Blue Moon Of Kentucky' was one of the first songs recorded by a young Elvis Presley at Sun.

The other new key element in the 30s was so vital that it even changed the name of the music from hillbilly to country and western, thanks to the growth of western swing in Texas and the enormous popularity of the Hollywood singing cowboys. While the singing cowboys may not have lasted long in relation to the history of country music, their legacy is enormous. The image of country music in the 90s owes a great deal to the western look of the Hollywood cowboys. Country had always relied on a bedrock of sentiment and nostalgia but the cowboys took it even further. Their wistful visions of times past, rolling prairies and tumbling tumbleweeds would stay with country music throughout enormous musical changes over the coming decades.

The singing cowboy must be one of the most unusual creations in Hollywood's history. The western movie may have treated the wild west with little regard for historical accuracy, but the singing cowboy pictures took the fantasy of the six-shooting hero to new extremes. It was the perfect antidote to the gloom of the American depression and the

Top, Tex Ritter was named "America's Most Beloved Cowboy" and made 85 westerns between 1936–1945, as well as frequently winning box office popularity polls.

Opposite, Bill Monroe, the father of bluegrass. An expert mandolin player, Monroe pioneered a whole musical style, thereby establishing himself as one of the most original figures of country music.

Left, Bill Monroe (centre) with his brother Charlie and Byron Parker (left). Still a regular at the Opry, Monroe remains a model of technical excellence.

fantasy cowboys took hold not just in America but across the world. The trend started when John Wayne took the part of Singin' Sandy, the first singing cowboy (though his voice was dubbed), in a dubious Republic quickie. Ken Maynard starred in several movies, but it was Gene Autry who set the genre on its way.

Autry, from Tioga Springs, Texas, had a credible musical record. In his early days he appeared on the Will Rogers show performing a pretty close impersonation of Jimmie Rodgers. His recording of 'That Silver-Haired Daddy Of Mine' in 1931 sold more than five million copies. In Tulsa he perfected his cowboy singer image and had his first western hit with 'The Yellow Rose Of Texas' in 1934. Mascot Pictures picked him up and tried him out in a Ken Maynard film entitled *In Old Santa Fe*. It was to be the first of over one hundred movies. Autry was an overnight success. His affable humble image and pleasant country singing voice caught on immediately. The best of the many movies he made were *Tumbling Tumbleweeds* (1935), *Oh Susanna* (1936) and *Melody Ranch* (1940). No fool as a businessman, he established himself as a marketing vehicle, ending up with an enormous business empire which included TV, radio and publishing companies and even part ownership of the Los Angeles Angels baseball team.

The next well-known singing cowboy, Roy Rogers, filled Autry's shoes while Autry was off the circuit in the Army Air Corps. Like Autry, Rogers had a sound musical background. His real name was Leonard Slye and he first found success alongside Bob Nolan and Tim Spencer as The Sons Of The Pioneers. Rogers' film career was established with his first western *Under Western Skies*, where he replaced Autry (who would not perform for the money offered). Eventually he made eighty-eight movies and became one of the most popular movie stars in Hollywood history. He went on to TV fame with a long-running series and continues to work even in his 80s. Another singing cowboy, Tex Ritter, never really matched the film successes of Autry and Rogers, but he eventually became a top-selling country artist. He made 58 singing cowboy movies, though it was his recording of the Academy Award-winning theme tune to the film *High Noon* that made him a bona fide star.

Left and inset, The life of the cowboy inspired the idealised and nostalgic singing cowboy films of the 30s. These popular but stylized western heroes were to colour country music for decades to come.

Right, Marty Robbins. Impossible to pigeonhole, Robbins played in a variety of country styles and achieved success with all of them. He made a final appearance in Clint Eastwood's *Honky Tonk Man* shortly before he died.

Opposite, top, Bob Wills (centre) guests on Billy Gray's television series *Music Country Style*, with western swing bandleader Dewey Groom. Gray (right) formerly worked with Hank Thompson.

Above, Three country music legends, Faron Young, Marty Robbins and George Jones, join forces on a Nashville country music television show.

Opposite, bottom, Uncle Dave Macon, "The Dixie Dewdrop", with the Delmore Brothers, Alton and Rabon. Macon was the Grand Ole Opry's first singer.

Although the singing cowboy era ended as abruptly as it started, the western influence in country music continued. Marty Robbins, who could feature in several genres in country music as he recorded pop and mainstream during a long career, hit the headlines in 1959 with 'El Paso', a western story song that spawned imitations and led Robbins himself to record two top-selling Gunfighter Ballads albums. Robbins himself was a mainstay in country music until his death in 1982, just after being elected to the Country Music Hall Of Fame.

While the singing cowboys provided a nostalgic escape from the rigours of 30s America, the southwesterners opted to dance their troubles away. Western swing, another of the many components of country music, originated in Texas and Oklahoma. The numerous cultural groups who had settled in these states imparted various musical influences into a country format that has remained solid to this day. Western swing absorbed a plethora of styles, but was essentially live dance music. The big band sound, Dixieland jazz, hoedowns, ballads and cowboy laments were all fused together to provide a joyful dance music, perfected for the popular two-step. The musicianship was impecc-

Right, George Jones, the leading honky-tonk singer, with Ernest Tubb. Although his personal dramas have hit the headlines, the 'Possum' remains a country legend.

Opposite, Patsy Montana, was the first female country singer to have a million-selling record with "I Want To Be A Cowboy's Sweetheart", released in 1935.

Below, Ernest Tubb was one of the original honky-tonk pioneers, who later made his mark with his famous Nashville record stores.

able, with some of the era's top instrumentalists, many from a jazz background, experimenting within the simple country format.

Bob Wills was the King of western swing, having started as a fiddler at dances in the Fort Worth region. His Texas Playboys came to typify and perfect the style and repertoire of western swing. The instrumental line-up was more daring than that of any other type of country music. Wills used guitars, fiddle, banjo, piano, drums, electric lead guitar and steel guitar. He recorded for several labels and had hits with such memorable tunes as 'Spanish Two-Step', 'Steel Guitar Rag', 'San Antonio Rose', 'Take Me Back To Tulsa' and 'Home In San Antone'.

While Texas provided swing, it was also home of yet another strain of country music, honky-tonk. This achieved prominence in the 40s with the likes of Ernest Tubb and Hank Williams, but its roots are firmly planted in the depression era. Early honky-tonk numbers like 'Honky-Tonk Blues' by Al Dexter and 'Born To Lose' by Ted Daffan pre-empted the themes of loss and loneliness

that would proliferate in the social upheaval of the 40s. Far from having the gospel and religious background of the southeastern mountain music that characterized the Grand Ole Opry, honky-tonk was born in the western oilfield roadhouses. It was drinking music, at times loud and raucous, at others maudlin, laced with a cryin' in the beer whimsy. The style leaned on steel guitar, electric rocking guitar and vocals that teetered on the edge of heartbreak.

It was Ernest Tubb who embodied the new style, moving away from the purity of sweet old-time country towards a much tougher and harsher sound. Tubb started as a Jimmie Rodgers-style blues yodeller, and indeed his first recordings were tributes to Rodgers. By the 40s his voice could no longer reach the high notes and he settled into a rougher style which perfectly suited his songwriting talents. Suddenly he found fame with the downbeat 'Walking The Floor Over You' and honky-tonk was born, a musical style that would change country music for ever once a certain Hank Williams had cut his teeth and a few records in the honky-tonk style had sold millions.

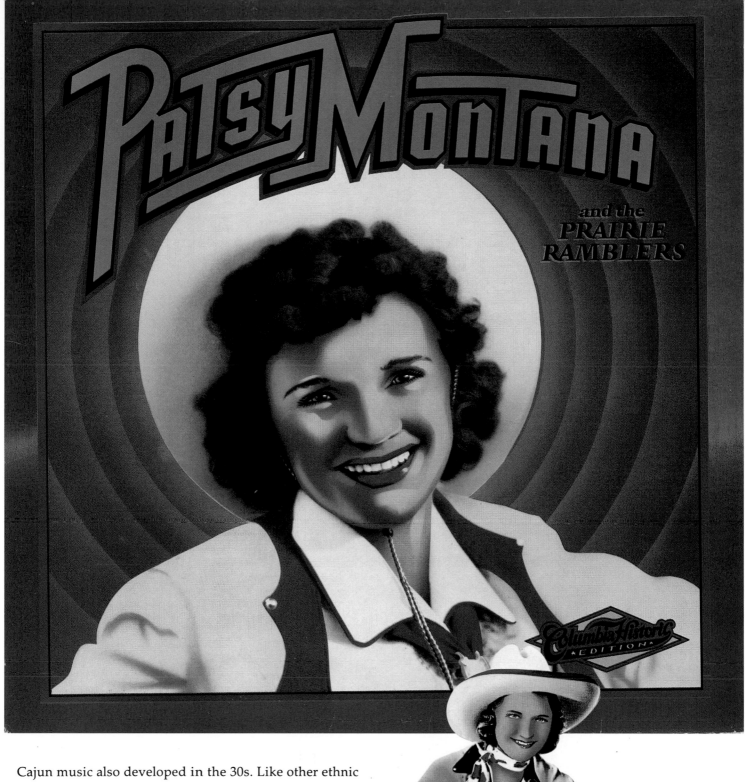

Cajun music also developed in the 30s. Like other ethnic music forms, it had roots that went way back, but during this period the Louisiana swamp sound, heavily dominated by the accordion and a driving beat, came to national prominence. The Hackberry Ramblers, who merrily mixed other styles with a cajun core, sang in both English and French and spread the cajun sound across America.

The 30s were truly creative years for country and western music. The business elements were being rapidly developed, numerous variations of the music were being cross-fertilized, and country was shaking off its tag as backwoods hillbilly music. It may have been disrupted by World War II, but everything was in place. All country needed was a superstar. And then came Hank Williams.

Hank Wil
MEMORIAL

M-G-M Long Playing 33⅓ r.p.m. Record.

2
Country Comes of Age

Ask almost any contemporary artist for a handful of musical influences and the chances are that the name of Hank Williams will pop out first. He burst on to the country scene like a whirlwind, quickly becoming a national superstar, an incredibly prolific songwriter, one of the finest ever performers and a romantic icon epitomizing the hard-living, hard-loving wild man. He died of alcohol abuse at just twenty-nine years of age. Originally he came from Alabama and his own musical heroes were Roy Acuff and Ernest Tubb. Equally at home with religious sentiment or with the cheatin' song, Hank Williams' voice came to speak for everyone.

Without Williams it is very possible that country music, however innovative and popular it had become by the 40s, would have remained in hicksville. Williams changed all that. A pale, lanky man dressed in white suit and cowboy hat, he had a stage presence and songwriting skills that

After he has become a star Hank Williams, Jr. is visited by his hometown girl friend Shelly Fabares.

MGM presents "A TIME TO SING" In PANAVISION® And METROCOLOR

Previous page, One of the first albums responsible for keeping Hank Williams' music alive. As his records have continued to sell, his classic songs are still recorded by contemporary artists.

Previous page, top, Hank Williams and his wife Audrey. Behind the music was a stormy relationship that led to a divorce shortly before Hank's death, and years of subsequent litigation and court battles.

Top right, Hank Williams with his son Randall Hank, nicknamed "Bocephus" but better known as Hank Jr., who eventually fought off the shadow of his father to emerge as a country superstar in the 70s and 80s (above).

were forerunners of the pop formats of the future. At twelve he won a song-writing competition, and just two years later had his own band, The Drifting Cowboys. They played honky-tonks and dances, and won spots on radio shows, but nothing really happened until the mid 40s when, after failing an audition for the Grand Ole Opry, he won a writing contract with Acuff Rose, the most important music publishing company in country music. Singing for the most part in the Acuff style, Williams did not stand out as a singer, but when Fred Rose heard Hank perform 'Honky-Tonkin' he immediately arranged a record deal with a major label.

Hank Williams would never look back. Two years later, with 'Lovesick Blues' high in the charts, he played his first show on the Opry. He received a standing ovation and six encores, and as he sat in his dressing-room the applause continued for a full five minutes. The Opry naturally enough made him a member, though even at that point some executives were more than concerned about the singer's wayward lifestyle. In a year Williams was the top draw in country. His songs ruled the airwaves – 'Long Gone Lonesome Blues' (1950), 'Why Don't You Love Me' (1950), 'Moaning The Blues' (1950) and 'Cold, Cold Heart' (1951). Pop artists like Tony Bennett began looking for Williams' songs to record. But it was all too much. He divorced his wife, added too many pills to his alcohol diet and died in the back of a car on the way to a gig on New

Left, Hank Williams put country music on the map, brought sexuality to his stage shows and lived the Outlaw's life long before Waylon and Willie tried it. He died on New Years Day 1953, still not yet 30.

Below, Poster for the show Hank Williams never gave. He died in the backseat of his Cadillac on the way to Canton.

"IF THE GOOD LORD'S WILLING, AND THE CREEK DON'T RISE" . . I'LL SEE YOU AT

Canton MEMORIAL AUD.
NEW YEAR'S DAY 1953
GRAND OLE OPRY
PRESENTS
IN PERSON

HANK WILLIAMS
AND HIS DRIFTING COWBOYS

Hatch Show Print Nashville, Tenn.

Year's Day in 1953. He was just twenty-nine. His importance, however, would live far longer. As Fred Rose's son Wesley stated, 'Hank was the first writer to make country music, national music'.

As country music developed its first superstar, so Nashville was fast building up its status as the business headquarters of country music. The Grand Ole Opry was the initial raison d'être for country musicians to head into town and, as the numbers increased, so the industry naturally came into existence. The Grand Ole Opry was booking its own talent, because there was no one else around to handle the task, while Acuff-Rose Music, created by Opry star Roy Acuff and songwriter Fred Rose in 1942, became the first business operation to set up shop. Other music publishing houses followed, including Hill Music and Range Music (later to merge as Hill & Range), and Southern Music, established in New York in 1927 by

pioneering talent scout Ralph Peer. Country recordings, however, were still being handled in New York or some other regional office. Decca Records, under the auspices of Paul Cohen, were the first label to record hillbilly artists in Nashville. They started in the spring of 1945 with artists such as Red Foley, Ernest Tubb and Kitty Wells, and began putting Nashville on the map as a recording centre. Owen Bradley, a pianist who became leader of Nashville's WSM radio orchestra, later assumed full responsibility for the country recordings when Cohen moved on to Coral Records.

In the meantime RCA, which had already enjoyed success thanks to the likes of Jimmie Rodgers, the Carter Family, Sons Of The Pioneers, Bill Monroe and Bill Boyd, among others, still continued to handle its country music productions from New York. Steve Shoals travelled regularly to Nashville to supervise the recordings, until his schedules became so busy that he handed some of his duties over to a young guitarist signed to the label, Chet Atkins. The label's biggest postwar success, and one of country music's all-time most successful artists, was Eddy Arnold, who first caught the public's attention on the Opry as a member of Pee Wee King's Golden West Cowboys. Launching his RCA career in 1946 with *All Alone In This*

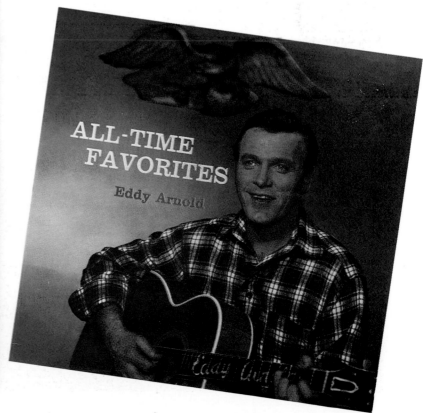

Webb Pierce and his Swimming Pool

Previous page, centre, The
Grand Ole Opry is part of the
Opryland complex, which
houses WSM radio, the
Nashville Network and a
fullblown theme park, as well
as the Opryland Hotel, one of
the largest and grandest hotels
in America.

Previous page, bottom, Eddy
Arnold, the best-selling
country music artist of all time.
Always adaptable, he started
out as one of Pee Wee King's
Golden West Cowboys before
embracing pop with the
Nashville Sound.

Above, One of the biggest
stars of the 50s and 60s, Webb
Pierce built himself a guitar-
shaped swimming pool. He
ran into trouble with the city
government in the 70s,
however, when he opened his
doors to the public and caused
traffic jams in his Nashville
neighbourhood.

World Without You he had, within a year, sold nearly three
million records. Two decades later Arnold was still going
strong as a mainstay of the Nashville Sound.

In July 1950 Capitol Records became the first major label
to base its country director in Nashville, and it was this
label that at the earlier urging of many of its west coast
artists (including Tex Ritter, Cliffie Stone and Eddie Dean)
first adopted the term 'country' rather than hillbilly', a
move quickly followed by Decca Records. By June 1949
Billboard began listing its popularity charts under the
heading of 'country' or 'country and western'. Columbia
Records set up its Nashville offices as late as 1961, with
British-born Don Law heading up the operation and shar-
ing recording responsibilities with another British expatri-
ate 'Uncle' Art Satherley, who first earned his reputation in
the business as a field scout during the 1920s.

Not surprisingly, new stars emerged. Country was more
popular than ever, Williams was a significant role model
and Nashville looked a likely place to find success. Webb
Pierce, a musical cousin of Williams, played it hard and

loud. His 'Slowly' (1954) is said to be the first country hit to feature pedal steel guitar. He perfected bar-room music, his gruff nasal vocals giving credibility to his downbeat honky-tonk tunes. He sold millions of records throughout the 50s, helped other artists like Faron Young and Floyd Cramer on their way and built himself a guitar-shaped swimming-pool in his Nashville home.

Faron Young made his name with a gentler strain of honky-tonk. His career rocketed after the success of 'Goin' Steady' (1953) and by 1960 he had achieved twenty hits. He hit the top of the pop charts in 1961 with 'Hello Walls' and ten years later found worldwide success with 'It's Four In The Morning'. Lefty Frizzell surfaced in the dance-halls of Texas and influenced a whole generation of singers with his idiosyncratic vocals. His voice was heartbreaking; he drawled and looped around his own catchy melodies. 'If You've Got Money I've Got The Time' established Frizzell as a star in 1950 and he chalked up around thirty hits in the next twenty years. Frizzell's career suffered because of a severe drink problem and he died in 1975 at forty-seven.

Ray Price's early sound was close to that of his hero, Hank Williams, partly due to the fact that his Cherokee Cowboys band was formed from the remnants of Williams' Drifting Cowboys. Like the best of the honky-tonkers, Price was from Texas. Although he would later become something of a crooner, his early success was pure honky-

Above, Tennessee Ernie Ford was one of the most popular country stars on the west coast. His biggest hit was Merle Travis's 'Sixteen Tons'. He had his own NBC television show and later concentrated on gospel recording.

Left, Lefty Frizzell – one of the finest singers of his generation and a major influence on numerous country stars, including Merle Haggard – was dogged by a terrible drink problem.

tonk. His first number one, 'Crazy Arms', was tough, spare and rhythmic, with fiddle soaring in the background. His classic from 1959, 'Heartaches By The Number', had steel guitar in the mix. Price sailed through the 60s with a softer sound, amassing record sales by the million, but his early records were classics all. He also played a major role in helping the careers of Willie Nelson, Roger Miller, Johnny Paycheck and steel guitarist Buddy Emmons.

No mention of honky-tonk is complete without the greatest honky-tonk vocalist of them all, George Jones. Yet another larger than life character, he has had a career dogged by controversy, drinking binges and irresponsible behaviour, but as a singer and vocal stylist he has nobody in country music to match him. Jones, also from Texas, began as a Hank Williams imitator and made his recording début on Starday Records with a top five hit, 'Why Baby Why?' He then rattled off a series of classic tears-in-the-beer tracks, 'White Lightning', 'She Thinks I Still Care', 'Tender Years' and many more. Jones' familiar singing

Right, The early George Jones, personified by a crew-cut and 100% genuine honky-tonk recordings on his début label, Starday Records, during the 50s.

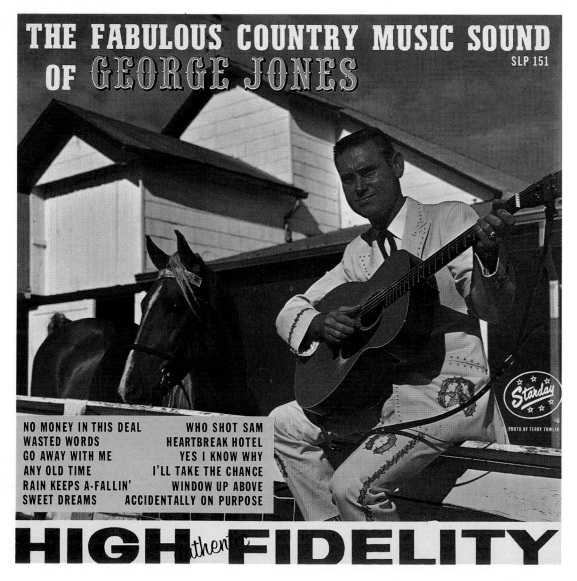

THE FABULOUS COUNTRY MUSIC SOUND OF GEORGE JONES

SLP 151

NO MONEY IN THIS DEAL
WASTED WORDS
GO AWAY WITH ME
ANY OLD TIME
RAIN KEEPS A-FALLIN'
SWEET DREAMS

WHO SHOT SAM
HEARTBREAK HOTEL
YES I KNOW WHY
I'LL TAKE THE CHANCE
WINDOW UP ABOVE
ACCIDENTALLY ON PURPOSE

PHOTO BY TERRY TOMLIN

HIGH then FIDELITY

Left, Hank Thompson was originally a radio cowboy, Hank the Hired Hand, before joining Capitol Records. The first country musician to perform in Las Vegas, his music has kept the western sound alive.

Below, Kitty Wells, the first female country singer to achieve real success in Nashville, opened the doors for countless other women artists.

style – a pained grimace, sliding notes and wild whining delivery – marks him out as one of the true originals in country music. The fact that his life has been just as colourful and traumatic as his music makes his position as a bona fide artist all the more credible. While some sing, Jones feels every note. These days he is a living legend and a major influence on countless contemporary stars from Garth Brooks to Randy Travis.

While honky-tonk was a clear forerunner of rock and roll, it also had very firm ties with old-time country. The delivery and instrumentation may have been frantic but the vocal style and high emotional delivery were pure country. And while Williams created a style, he also inspired a movement back to old-time country music, away from the jazz-tinged western swing and baritone ballads of the cowboys. The traditional hillbilly sound resurfaced very strongly in the 50s, led by the first female star of country music, Kitty Wells. Johnny Wright's wife Muriel Deason, from Nashville, started singing a few songs at his gigs in the 40s under the stage-name of Kitty Wells. Her first recording, 'It Wasn't God Who Made Honky-Tonk Angels' (recorded as an answer song to Hank Thompson's 'The Wild Side Of Life') in 1952, brought her national acclaim. The sound was pure mountain country but the lyrics were strong and from a woman's point of view. Women have made up a considerable segment of the country market and with Wells women across America suddenly found a voice with which to identify.

As far as purity goes, few could match the brother duo of Charles and Ira Louvin. Their mandolin guitar double act was sensational in its passion and power. Their songs were hard-hitting, their singing high-pitched, eerie and spine-tingling. Throughout the 50s they kept the rich mountain sound alive, heavily influencing the Everly Brothers as well as later country rockers Emmylou Harris and Gram Parsons. Hank Snow also looked back into the country music past for his inspiration. An excellent guitarist, he pushed his very clear vocals to the front. His success started with 'I'm Movin' On' in 1950 and from that point he was a Nashville and country music stalwart, continuing to appeal while trends came and went and other artists fell by the wayside.

Country music in the 50s was in a healthy state. It was expanding rapidly, new artists were flooding in and it was finding a more solid voice that could embrace the numerous subdivisions of the country genre. Hank Williams had played a key role in giving country drive and passion with his highly literate version of honky-tonk. That excitement would be utilized by the rock and rollers and so would change the nature of country music for ever.

Rockabilly gave country music yet another injection of passion and fervour. It also brought a new, young audience and while the boom only lasted a short time before developing into rock and roll, the rockabilly style would

continue to be a part of country music right through to the 90s, when the clipped lead lines and driving beat are very much in evidence in the performances of country artists like Marty Stuart and Kelly Willis.

The rockabilly sound was small and compact, with lead guitar, drums, piano and slap bass as the key components. It had a hard back beat, the instrumental breaks were short and snappy, and the vocals adapted the honky-tonk style with an amalgam of yelps and wails. It was a product of Southern music, black and white in equal parts. The lyrics and vocals came straight from country music, the rhythm and pace from rhythm and blues and also bluegrass. What also emerged was an aggression of performance that made the music compelling to the blossoming teenage movement in America. This was young people's music – and it had its very own star. It was the combination of Sun Records and Elvis Presley that brought rockabilly into the public's imagination. Bill Haley may have recorded rock and roll records prior to Elvis, but Presley, The Hillbilly Cat

Opposite, top, Hank Snow, a country star for many years in Canada, found fame in the United States in 1949. A regular at the Opry, he was elected to the Hall of Fame in 1979. Chet Atkins, also a member, stands by.

Opposite, far left, *Second Fiddle To A Steel Guitar*, just one of a mass of country music B-movies that emerged during the 50s and 60s, just as the rock 'n' roll audience had their own low budget productions.

Above, *Country Music On Broadway*, another country music "quickie" production, this time with Ferlin Husky heading up the celebrity cast.

Opposite, top, Elvis Presley,
The King, combined country
music and blues to give
America rock and roll. He
never abandoned his country
roots and continued to record
in Nashville throughout the
70s until his death in 1977.

Right, Elvis Presley in full
flow, backed by The
Jordanaires, the vocal quartet
who accompanied him on
many of his recording
sessions, and in his movies.

Below, The Elvis Presley
Museum and Gift Store is still
a major attraction in Nashville,
where fans can buy assorted
mementos.

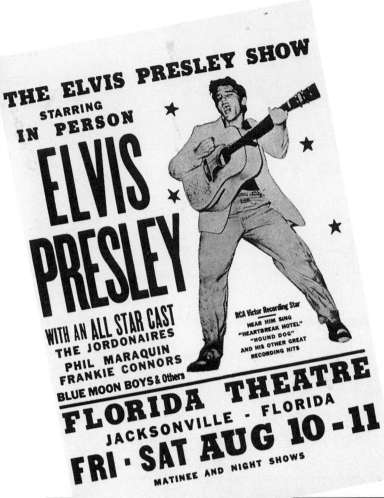

THE ELVIS PRESLEY SHOW
STARRING
IN PERSON
ELVIS PRESLEY
WITH AN ALL STAR CAST
THE JORDONAIRES
PHIL MARAQUIN
FRANKIE CONNORS
BLUE MOON BOYS & Others

RCA Victor Recording Star
HEAR HIM SING
"HEARTBREAK HOTEL"
"HOUND DOG"
AND HIS OTHER GREAT
RECORDING HITS

FLORIDA THEATRE
JACKSONVILLE · FLORIDA
FRI · SAT AUG 10 - 11
MATINEE AND NIGHT SHOWS

as he was already known in 1954, gave rockabilly its drive and passion. His early Sun recordings – 'That's All Right Mama', 'Good Rockin' Tonight', 'I Don't Care If The Sun Don't Shine', 'Mystery Train' and a host more – ignited the rockabilly flame.

Sun Records, the brain-child of Sam Phillips, threw up three more country and rockabilly performers who alongside Presley were known as the million dollar quartet. The three, Carl Perkins, Jerry Lee Lewis and Johnny Cash, would take their places as rock music pioneers as well as country legends. Jack Clement, who engineered many of their records at the famed Sun Studios in Memphis, recalls a 'great sense of abandon and excitement about everything the boys did. None of us really knew what we were doing but it felt right at the time. They all had different styles but for a while it all had that rockabilly feel. It was the spontaneity that made it, I think. I recall Jerry Lee coming in and playing "Great Balls Of Fire" through to us. We recorded it on the second take and that was that. A hit and a classic.' Johnny Cash's Sun Records provided the public's first taste of that deep booming voice and the simple clipped backings of his Tennessee Two (Luther Perkins

Opposite, top, Harold Jenkins, who changed his name to Conway Twitty, outside his home in Twitty City, a tourist attraction at Hendersonville, Tennessee. Loretta Lynn, The Coalminer's Daughter, had a successful run of duets with Twitty.

and Marshall Grant). It was a sound that Cash carried into his country music heyday of the 60s.

Carl Perkins was arguably the definitive rockabilly artist. He was originally signed to Sun as a country singer, and his bluesy vocals and innovative electric guitar playing made him perfect for the emerging youth market. In 1956 he recorded his own 'Blue Suede Shoes', a hit on both pop and country charts, but a near-fatal car accident prevented him from cashing in. Presley recorded the song, became an international superstar, and Perkins never quite found the public acclaim his talent deserved.

Jerry Lee Lewis, The Killer, was the dangerous edge of rockabilly. Armed with his piano, Jerry Lee was a crazed man. The voice roared, the feet danced and his head jerked in rhythm. His unpredictability on stage gave promoters and concert organizers headaches by the dozen, but Lewis created a new musical style. He was rockabilly but he was many other things too. His piano playing was truly innovative, fusing jazz, boogie-woogie, honky-tonk, ragtime and country into his own, instantly recognizable sound. He was also capable of country tenderness in softer ballads. Other Sun artists tried to follow the success of the leading four, Charlie Rich and Carl Mann among them, but none reached the heights of those initial pioneers.

Above, Jerry Lee Lewis, The Killer, has worked both inside and outside country music throughout his long and turbulent career.

Previous page, bottom, Rockabilly legends, Carl Perkins, Jerry Lee Lewis, Roy Orbison and Johnny Cash, join forces for the 1985 album, "Class of 55".

Right, Buddy Holly, the singer-songwriter from Lubbock, Texas, was a kingpin of rock and roll, but his debt to country music remained very real. He died in a plane crash in 1959.

Opposite, bottom, Brenda Lee in her early rocking days.

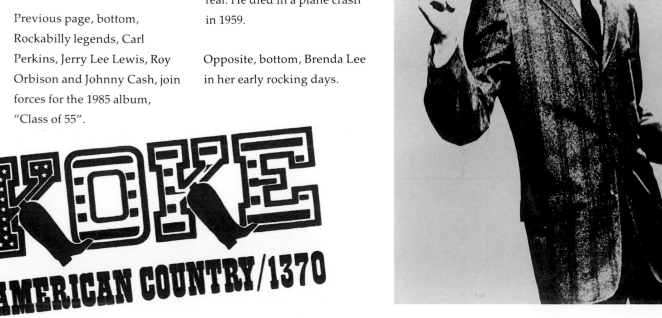

KOKE
AMERICAN COUNTRY/1370

Sun and Memphis wasn't the only place where the country sound was being beefed up into a primitive rock and roll. Conway Twitty (real name Harold Jenkins), later a major force in country music, was initially inspired by the Sun sound and had major hits with 'It's Only Make Believe' and 'Mona Lisa'. In Texas, Lubbock to be exact, Buddy Holly gave his own brand of country music a rocking beat. He never scored a country hit, but he played a major role in shaping the future of country and rock. Wanda Jackson and Brenda Lee ensured that women took their place in rockabilly history. The sound of the Everly Brothers was gentler than that of the Sun artists, but they also cleverly melted country with drive and won the hearts of millions of American teenagers. Don and Phil, from Kentucky, started out as pure mountain country but, in tandem with songwriters extraordinaires, Felice and Boudleaux Bryant, they notched up a string of country-flavoured pop hits, highlighted by 'Bye Bye Love' (1957), 'Wake Up Little Susie' (1958) and 'All I Have To Do Is Dream' (1959).

Top, The Nashville skyline, as viewed from Music Row.

Above, The Country Music Hall of Fame.

Opposite, Printers Alley, in downtown Nashville, the town's original tourist area, where several artists owned their own nightclubs.

The dynamic success of rockabilly and its offshoot rock and roll had a powerful effect on country music. Many pure country singers fell by the wayside in the rockabilly avalanche. Older artists did not appeal to the new young crowd. Nashville had been shaken by the Memphis effect and felt itself in retreat. Something had to be done to revitalize country in the light of rock and roll. The formula became known as the Nashville Sound.

As country entered the 60s it was in a precarious state. Years of innovation and creativity had been challenged by a music that ironically had grown out of country. Nashville needed to sell more records, it wanted a newer, cleaner image and a crisper, more contemporary sound. Violins replaced fiddles, the banjo disappeared and the steel guitar took a back seat. The producers took advantage of the new technology that made pop singers like Sinatra and Tony Bennett sound pure and sophisticated. They employed background vocals and string sections to make music which would appeal to an older audience, to listeners not terribly interested in the wailing of rock and roll. One man given a lot of credit for creating the Nashville Sound is

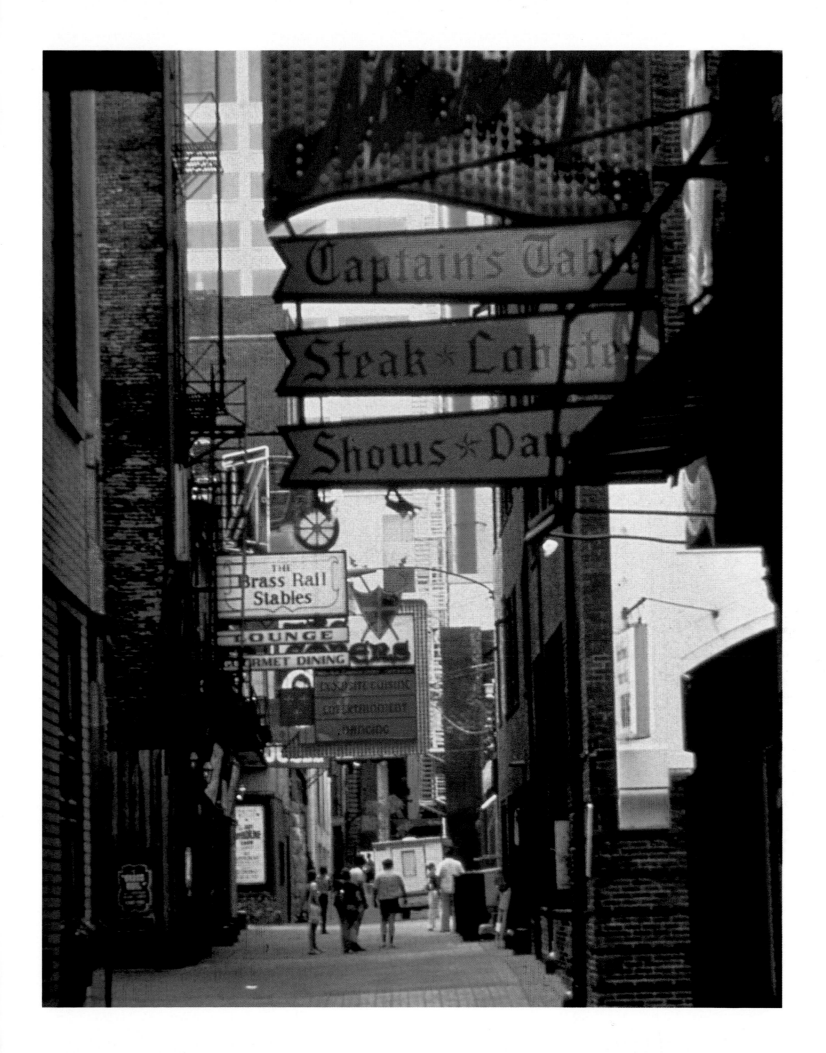

Chet Atkins. Atkins himself is reticent about his legendary status. 'It was something that happened. I was in the right place at the right time. Because I was educated in music and understood orchestration I was the one that understood what the record companies wanted.' An inspired guitarist (Mark Knopfler of Dire Straits cites him as still the best in the world), Atkins fell into production by accident. 'They didn't really have producers in the late 50s. I recorded Elvis in Nashville but I wasn't given any producer's credit. That's how it was. But I got a name around town, recorded a hell of a lot of people. It wasn't that I wanted to get rid of the old country sound but we needed something different. I recorded some Don Gibson tracks with the old musical line-up and nothing happened. I tried it differently, with me on electric guitar and more of a pop sound and his career took off. We needed something new. I'd always listened to all kinds of music. I love doing classical concerts, so it was natural for me to develop that cleaner, less country sound.'

For some artists the new style did not work; for others it was perfect. Eddy Arnold was probably the first country artist to capitalize on the new styles of the 60s. He moved from hard country, where he was known as the Tennessee Plowboy, to tuxedo-toting smooth crooner. He worked perfectly in the burgeoning middle-of-the-road market, had several hit records with songs like 'What's He Doing To My World?', 'Make The World Go Away' and 'Then You Can Tell Me Goodbye', appeared in his own long-running TV series and sold in excess of fifty million records over his

Above, Skeeter Davis, who perfectly adapted her music to the Nashville sound of the 60s and became one of the biggest stars of the decade.

Right, Chet Atkins and Mark Knopfler doing what both do best. Knopfler, from the rock band, Dire Straits, has called Atkins the finest guitarist of them all. Atkins' response is, 'Well, if that's what he says'.

career. Clearly Nashville's belief that it could create a successful alternative to the rock and roll market had a good deal of credibility.

While Arnold may have got in first, it was Jim Reeves who made the Nashville Sound his own. Reeves was the epitome of the new country. His voice was velvet smooth, his look clean cut and sophisticated. After a few country hits he made the big time under Chet Atkins' direction with the classic 'He'll Have To Go', a recording that perfectly typifies the new brand of country music. The emotion is still up front but the delivery is laid back, considered and exquisitely smooth and sweet. Reeves himself did not live long enough to enjoy his massive success, dying in a plane crash in 1964, but he was a major player in forging a new strain of country music, the easy-listening sound that still proves popular today.

If the Nashville Sound was about balance and compromise, it found perfection with Patsy Cline. Initially a straight country singer from Virginia, she teamed up with producer

Opposite, top left, Don Gibson spent many years struggling for recognition before becoming a leading member of the "Nashville Sound".

Top and above, Jim Reeves, known as 'Gentleman Jim', the smooth sound of country music, made *Kimberley Jim*, his only movie, in South Africa.

Owen Bradley, who brought out pop qualities in her performances, to make some breathtaking records. Like Reeves, Cline also died young in a plane crash, but before that she recorded a body of work that matches anything in popular music. 'Walkin' After Midnight' set her on her way in 1957 and by 1959 she was the new Queen of Country, with songs like 'I Fall To Pieces', 'Crazy' and 'She's Got You'. Alongside Reeves, Cline brought country music to mass public acceptance.

The 60s decade was all about change, not just in America as a nation but in entertainment and the arts. The country cried out for innovation, for new experiences. Already country music had shifted gear, ready to infiltrate the growing world of pop music. Crossover was to be the order of these years, with music of all styles borrowed from every other genre. The Beatles took the nation by storm with their cross-fertilization of rock and roll, blues and country. American pop groups like The Byrds and The Lovin' Spoonful nodded a head in Nashville's direction with some of their arrangements. Nashville itself would embrace the rock and folk stars like Bob Dylan and John Denver. New stars like Johnny Cash and Glen Campbell changed their music to suit the eclectic tastes of the 60s. This was the time when Nashville began trying to drop the country and western moniker in favour of just country.

The Nashville Sound had such an influence in the early 60s that a group of artists emerged all loosely basing their styles on the sounds created by Chet Atkins. Not surprisingly, with Atkins running RCA records in Nashville many of these artists recorded for RCA. Hank Locklin, although he had been recording since the 40s, found his heyday in the 60s with country pop hits like 'Please Help Me I'm Falling' (1960). Connie Smith plunged herself into the new polished sound and struck gold in 1964 with 'Once A Day'. David Houston scored countless hits in the decade, none better than his recording of 'Almost Persuaded' in 1966. Conway Twitty moved gracefully from an early rocking career to the more sophisticated Nashville of the 60s. George Hamilton IV started out as a rock'n'roller before establishing himself as a country star in the 60s with Atkins at the helm. His major hit was 'Abilene' in 1963. Hamilton played an important role in opening up the country sound. He regularly looked further afield than Nashville for his material, being among the first to record songs by Joni Mitchell and Gordon Lightfoot. Bobby Bare, like Hamilton, started out as a rocker but he had a knack for moving with the times and scored heavily throughout the 60s with a softer sound. To prove his progressive thinking,

Opposite, Patsy Cline brought country music to a mass audience with her dramatic singing style.

Above, George Hamilton IV accidently had a brief career as a million-selling, pop teen idol before pursuing his true aims as a country music artist and achieving hits like "Abilene" and "Fort Worth, Dallas Or Houston".

in the 70s he was recording songs by the new breed of writers like Kris Kristofferson and Billy Joe Shaver.

Perhaps the most interesting exponent of smooth country music was Charley Pride. For Nashville, Pride represented a historical breakthrough: he was the first black performer to become a country superstar in what was traditionally a white music form. Chet Atkins, the man behind Pride's success, is adamant to this day, however, that there was no opposition to Pride on race grounds. 'We weren't sure what to do with Charley. It didn't matter to me that he was black. My Grandpa was a fierce anti-slavery campaigner but obviously I wondered what the reaction would be. We decided to put the first single out ("The Snakes Crawl At Night") with no fuss, no hype. People loved the record and when it became known that Charley was black they still loved the record and they loved him.' Pride scored several number ones by the end of the 60s and has continued to be one of the most popular entertainers in the genre. As he says, 'I'm an American singing American music, not a black man singing a white man's music'.

Above, Kris Kristofferson. A Rhodes scholar and an athlete, Kristofferson settled on Nashville as his spiritual home in the 60s. He worked as a janitor before finding success as a songwriter with tunes like 'Sunday Morning Comes Down' and 'Help Me Make It Through The Night'.

Country pop, however, was not the only key development in the 60s. The Country Music Association, founded in 1958 and backed by the industry, consolidated its position as a guiding light to country music in America. It spread country music via radio stations and television exposure. A Country Music Hall Of Fame was initiated in 1961, The Country Music Foundation in 1964 and organized network coverage for the annual country music CMA awards in 1968.

With this solid base, country could genuinely prosper and challenge the rock and pop markets, but it still needed fresh blood and superstars to keep its image contemporary and alive. Two of the most acclaimed country performers of all time emerged at this point, Loretta Lynn and Tammy Wynette. Both provided role models for the countless women performers who would follow them to Nashville and Loretta particularly gave a voice to the growing women's movement in the United States.

Loretta Lynn's rags to riches tale has been accurately documented in the movie *Coalminer's Daughter*. Encour-

Above, Loretta Lynn brought women's concerns to prominence in country music with controversial tunes like 'The Pill'.

Opposite, bottom, Charley Pride, a popular exponent of the Nashville Sound, proved that colour was unimportant in country music.

Below, Nashville, the home of country music, attracts tourists by the million.

Above, left, Loretta Lynn with Rhythm and Blues legend, Ray Charles, who made some impressive country recordings in his own right. Top, right, Loretta Lynn and Ernest Tubb on stage at the Opry.

aged to break out of poverty and into a singing career by her husband Mooney Lynn, she had a small hit with her first single 'Honky-Tonk Girl', a task achieved primarily by Mooney driving Loretta Lynn around as many radio stations as geography and time would allow. The single opened several doors, notably by winning the support of famed country producer Owen Bradley (the man behind Patsy Cline recordings). Her background and attitudes surfaced in her self-penned songs. Though by no means a militant feminist, Lynn was never going to place women in a secondary role to men. There was a spirit of sassy self-preservation running through her songs, defiant while never aggressive. 'Don't Come Home A'Drinkin' With Lovin' On Your Mind' was typical of her lyrical standpoint. Later she became bolder with the somewhat controversial song 'The Pill', which included the line 'Feelin' good is easy now 'cos I've got the Pill'.

Like Lynn, Tammy Wynette had several obstacles to overcome before she could become a country star. After an early marriage, several low-paid jobs and three children, she headed for Nashville, with the kids in the back of the

car. Luck followed when she got a break on the Porter Waggoner television show and hit the charts with 'I Don't Want To Play House'. In 1968 she recorded the biggest selling single by a female country artist, the anthem-like 'Stand By Your Man'. She has since sold millions of records, won numerous country awards and lived through traumatic times and publicized affairs of the heart with both George Jones and Burt Reynolds.

It was during the 60s too that Nashville firmly established itself as the home of the songwriter. With major publishing companies basing themselves there, an indus-

Above, George Jones, Tammy Wynette and Billy Sherill. A successful producer, Sherill took Wynette to the top with a sophisticated sound. Her duets with real-life husband, George Jones, caught the public imagination.

Below, The two faces of Willie Nelson. The short-haired version wrote hits like 'Crazy' for Patsy Cline, while the later incarnation saw Nelson in Texas, an Outlaw and a superstar.

Right, Singer/songwriter Bill Anderson turned his skills towards the kitchen, when he launched his chain of "Po Folks" restaurants. He is also a successful quiz host on the Nashville Network.

try grew up providing hit material for the army of country singers. The most successful writers of the late 50s were Felice and Boudleaux Bryant, a husband and wife team who wrote many Everly Brothers hits as well as the often recorded 'Rocky Top'. Harlan Howard, who is still one of Nashville's top writers, peaked in the 50s and 60s with songs like 'I Fall To Pieces' and 'Heartaches By The Number'. Others began as writers before hitting the boards themselves. Bill Anderson had songs cut by stars like Jim Reeves and Faron Young before making his own records. Mel Tillis wrote memorable tunes like 'Detroit City' and 'Ruby, Don't Take Your Love To Town' before making his own way in the 70s. Willie Nelson spent many a year toiling in an upstairs office coming up with songs like 'Crazy' for Patsy Cline before bursting on to the scene in the 70s as a solo act.

Nobody inspired the plethora of singer-songwriter who came to Nashville in the 60s more than towering country legend Johnny Cash. He had surfaced in the 50s at Sun Records with a country-flavoured rockabilly, but the 60s saw him at the peak of his powers. Aside from his no-nonsense approach and looming stage presence, the Man In Black set standards in songwriting that still remain

Previous page, Boudeleaux and Felice Bryant, arguably the most successful country-pop songwriting team ever, at home in Gatlinburg, Tennessee. They were elected into the Country Music Hall of Fame in 1991.

Above, June Carter and Johnny Cash, Waylon Jennings and Jessi Colter, the best of husband-and-wife teams.

Right, Johnny Cash became the voice of country music in the 60s.

today. As well as making a trail of hits in the 60s he moved country towards a rock ethos with some groundbreaking concept albums. *Ride This Train* looked at the legacy and legends of the railroads, *Bitter Tears* considered the treatment of the Indian, and *Ballads Of The True West* dwelt on prairie and cowboy matters. He brought his own Christian-based humanity into all the topics he covered. He campaigned for prison reform and recorded the acclaimed San Quentin live prison album in 1969. And all the time his lyrics spoke the truth as he saw it. Never one to take any political line, he treated every topic with fresh eyes, seeking out injustice and pain and damning inequalities with his lyrics. 'Well, to me that's what country music is all about. It really is the music of the people and while a lot of my songs have been pretty simple love songs, some of them are more outspoken. But there are things wrong in this country and I don't see how ignoring those things does any good. There are also many wonderful things about America and I think I celebrate those as well. If I had to label myself it would probably be as a songwriter. That gives me immense satisfaction, and I've been lucky enough to work with some of the great writers like Bob Dylan, Kris Kristofferson and Paul McCartney.'

Carnegie Hall Concert with **BUCK OWENS AND HIS BUCKAROOS**

stereo

A "Live" Recording Of Their Great Performance At The Famous New York Concert Hall

If Cash showed that country music did not have to obey convention and rules, then Roger Miller took full advantage with a barrage of witty, off-the-wall and perfectly crafted songs throughout the 60s. He started out in the late 50s, still heavily influenced by Hank Williams, and had modest success with some straight country songs. Ray Price recorded his 'Invitation To The Blues' and Ernest Tubb cut 'Half A Mind'. But in the mid 60s he threw all formulas aside and recorded a stream of songs that were unique, quirky and took country and pop audiences by

storm and by surprise. The titles are as left-field as the songs 'Dang Me', 'Chug A Lug', 'England Swings' and the classic 'King Of The Road'. He won eleven Grammy awards, sold millions of records and inspired others to loosen up the traditional country song format.

If Miller went for the surreal approach, then Tom T. Hall took a more literary angle for his new brand of country songwriting. The son of a preacher, Hall owed his success to his knack for observation and storytelling, his album titles reflecting that side of his craft – *I Witness Life*, *The Storyteller* and *The Rhymer And Other Five And Dimers*. His songs took the minutiae of life and made them broad. 'The Year That Clayton Delaney Died' is ostensibly about a small-town musician, but in Hall's capable hands it becomes a song about every struggling outsider.

Left and above, Buck Owens and his Buckaroos. Owens, the voice of California's Bakersfield sound, had a string of hits with a rougher edge than Nashville allowed. His concert at Carnegie Hall was the first held there by a country music artist.

State of California
GOVERNOR'S OFFICE
SACRAMENTO 95814

RONALD REAGAN
GOVERNOR

RECEIVED MAR 2 1 1972

March 14, 1972

Mr. Merle Ronald Haggard
P. O. Box 842
Bakersfield, California 93302

Dear Mr. Haggard:

After careful investigation of your case it has
been recommended to me that you be granted a
full and unconditional pardon.

I have considered the record and am satisfied
that yours is an appropriate case for executive
clemency. It is a great personal satisfaction
to me as Governor to make this acknowledgement
that you are deserving of favorable consideration.

Accordingly, I am enclosing the formal document
granting to you a full and unconditional pardon,
and with it I extend to you my best wishes for
your success and happiness.

Sincerely,

Ronald Reagan

RONALD REAGAN
Governor

Enclosure

CERTIFIED - RETURN RECEIPT REQUESTED

Above, Merle Haggard, the Okie from Muskogee, received a pardon in 1972 from Ronald Reagan, then governor of California, after serving two years and five months in San Quentin. While in jail he had been in the audience for Johnny Cash's San Quentin appearance.

Other stars got their breaks in the 60s – Waylon Jennings, Dolly Parton, Kris Kristofferson, Barbara Mandrell and so on – but their day would be the 70s. In the meantime, out on the west coast other developments in country music were proving every bit as influential as the consolidation of Nashville as the home of country. California had long been a bedrock of country music. Capitol Records in Los Angeles were well established in the 40s and signed such country stalwarts as Merle Travis, Tex Ritter and Tennessee Ernie Ford. In the 50s they had Hank Thompson, Ferlin Husky, Wanda Jackson and Faron Young. But California also generated its own sound and its own movement, Bakersfield. It was not a sound in the way that the Nashville Sound was easily identified – it was wilder than Nashville's output, more hard country, more fiddle and steel guitar. That country music would eventually turn into a major business in Los Angeles via country rock is due in no small measure to the thriving bounce of the Bakersfield sound.

The Oklahoma migrants who moved out to the promised land of California naturally took their lifestyle and music with them, hence the popularity of country music on the west coast. Artists like Wynn Stewart and Rose Maddox had very large and loyal followings, but it took Buck Owens to forge a whole movement. One of the highest-charting artists of the 60s, Owens was the catalyst for the whole west coast scene. He moved to Bakersfield from Texas in 1951, played guitar around town for some years and did not start singing until the end of the decade. Once he started recording, however, the hits just kept on coming – 'Above And Beyond', 'Excuse Me' (1960), 'Act Naturally' (1963), 'Tiger By The Tail' and 'Buckaroo' (1965) and 'Sam's Place' (1967). Buck Owens also had talent as a businessman and built a small entertainment empire which helped maintain the west coast sound. For Owens it was an antidote to the Nashville Sound. 'I didn't like some of the things they were doing. It was too sweet, too pop, if you will. I liked country music and that's what we played. And

Above, Glen Campbell, top country-pop "crossover" entertainer, on stage with Carl Jackson, one of the world's finest banjo players and a former member of the Campbell band.

Right, Glen Campbell made country hits in Los Angeles style and had a successful television show for many years. He also invented the Glen Campbell guitar.

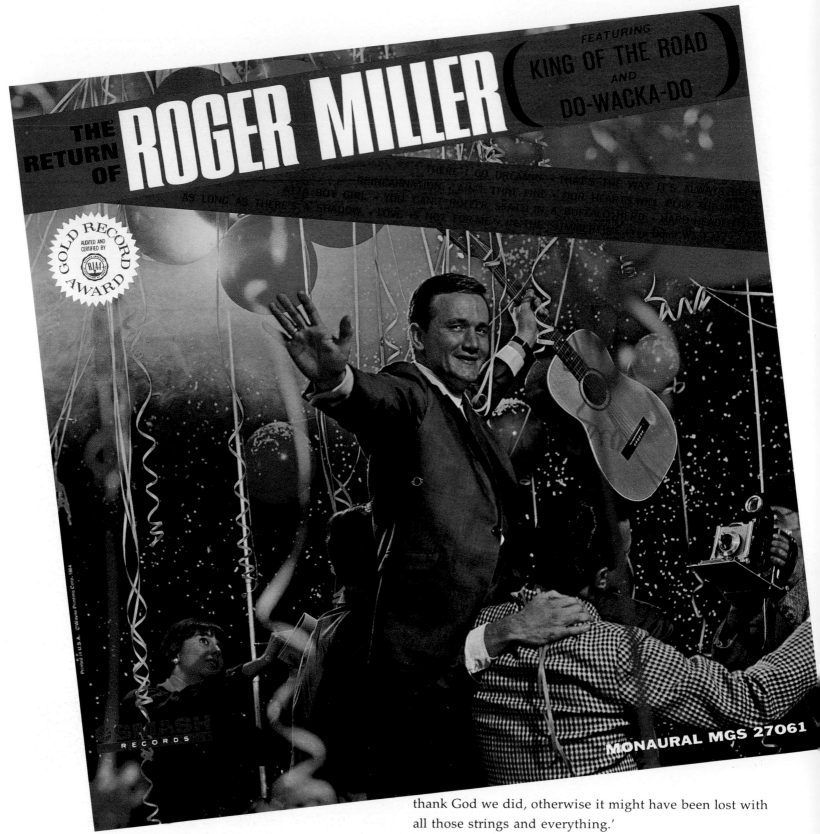

THE
RETURN OF **ROGER MILLER**

FEATURING
KING OF THE ROAD
AND
DO-WACKA-DO

GOLD RECORD AWARD
AUDITED AND CERTIFIED BY RIAA

MONAURAL MGS 27061

SMASH RECORDS

thank God we did, otherwise it might have been lost with all those strings and everything.'

But Owens could only be a pioneer if others followed his example. Fortunately they did. Merle Haggard's temperament perfectly suited the maverick world of California country. A loner and never afraid to speak his mind, Haggard would have had great difficulty surviving in the conformist environment of 60s Nashville. The son of dust-

Above, Roger Miller, whose songs brought wit and word-play to the Nashville songwriting world.

Left, Roger Miller changed the nature of country songwriting with a series of witty, off-the-wall hits.

Below, Tom T. Hall, The Storyteller, pictured in the library at his home in Franklin, Tennessee.

bowl migrants (from Oklahoma to California), he spent his early years in trouble with the law, including two years at San Quentin. On settling down in Bakersfield, he got work as a guitarist with Wynn Stewart and eventually a recording contract with Capitol. Haggard's music had roots in folk story-telling, but over his long career he has played in almost every authentic branch of country music. He has recorded tributes to the Carter Family and Jimmie Rodgers, he has played Dixieland, western swing and cajun. But above all, he kept his country music hard and true while most around him were searching for pop crossover success. His own songs show a perceptive mind, his lyrics dealing mostly with life's woes. His biggest hit was 'Okie From Muskogee', which became something of a pro-Vietnam War cry, although Haggard to this day claims it was written with a good measure of irony. For Haggard, however, the song became something of a millstone, because he was seen as the archetypal pro-American country singer. Nixon even sent him a congratulatory letter. Haggard himself was never so black and white; indeed he had planned a song about an inter-racial love affair for his follow-up single to 'Okie' but Capitol balked at the idea. Haggard's mournful vocals, dexterous guitar work and uncompromising and hard-hitting style have made him one of the most respected of all the postwar country artists.

The west coast was not blind to the success Nashville

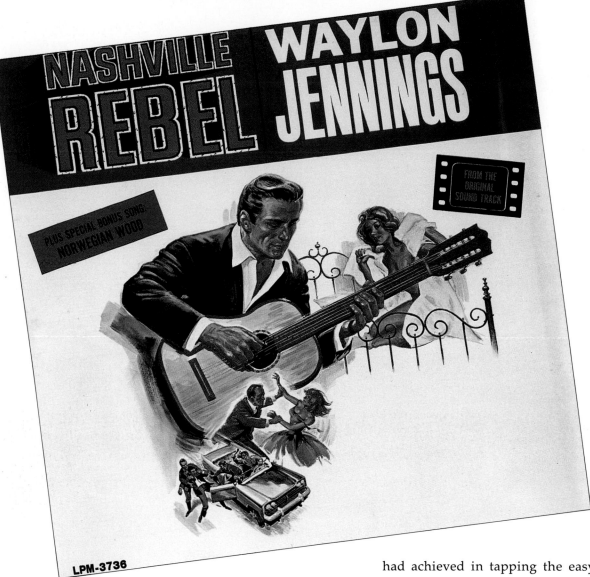

LPM-3736

Above, Waylon Jennings.
Long before the beard and
long hair made Jennings an
Outlaw, he liked to do things
his own way.

had achieved in tapping the easy-listening market. Two Hollywood artists, Glen Campbell and Roy Clark, fused country with a Hollywood polish and showbiz bent and found phenomenal success in all entertainment spheres from movies to television shows. Campbell won his initial musical reputation as one of the hottest guitarists on the Los Angeles session circuit. The work poured in, and during one year he played nearly 600 sessions for the likes of The Beach Boys, The Mamas and Papas, The Monkees and Frank Sinatra. Even so, there was an element of fortune in getting so many sessions. 'I remember some Sinatra sessions and the guy in charge of the orchestra didn't know too much about guitars, but they wanted that sound because it was the sound to have in the early 60s. I played twelve-string, which gave a bright ring, I could change key with a capo and they thought I had some magic sound. But it wasn't anything that any bar-room picker wouldn't have come up with.'

Campbell still yearned for solo recordings and in 1967 struck gold with John Hartford's 'Gentle On My Mind', a whimsical and emotive country folk number that Campbell

quickly made his own. He then recorded several Jimmy Webb compositions, 'Wichita Lineman', 'Galveston' and 'Where's The Playground Susie', before securing his own network television show and even a film role alongside John Wayne in *True Grit*. 'I don't know if I'm strictly a country singer,' says Campbell, 'but there's always been a country influence and a country sound in my voice. The great thing about country is that it's very emotional music and for me music has to be emotional or there's little sense in playing it. I can do all that clever jazz stuff but when a simple song breaks your heart that's when it all becomes absolutely compelling.'

Just as the Grand Ole Opry and radio developments had pushed country music into America's homes in the 20s and 30s, so television in the 60s proved a showcase for country performers. Campbell had his own Goodtime Hour, which was glitzy but highlighted several country artists. George Hamilton IV had a show, so did Johnny Cash, and then there was Hee Haw, a down-home country variety music show, a Laugh In for rural America. The long-time star of Hee Haw, Roy Clark, came out of California initially as a

Above, Gram Parsons (centre), one-time Byrd, friend of Keith Richards and a country music pioneer.

Right, Gram Parsons may have been a rich kid with a self-destructive edge, but his love of country music was very real.

highly respected guitarist. A natural entertainer, he guested on the Beverly Hillbillies television show before topping the charts himself in 1969 with Charles Aznavour's 'Yesterday When I Was Young'. Both Campbell and Clark pioneered the move for country performers to become all-round entertainers, a trend that grew in the 70s with artists like Dolly Parton, Kenny Rogers and Barbara Mandrell. They may have polished off some of the raw emotion of country but in turn they brought the style to an even wider audience.

With music in the turbulent 60s emerging as the single most powerful cultural art form, artists from all fields of popular music looked for ways to broaden their sound. The folk revival was in full swing in the early 60s, with artists like The Kingston Trio and Peter, Paul and Mary at the top of the charts. Musicians across America looked to folk music to inspire their writing in the rock idiom. The Byrds, one of the decade's major bands, beefed up Bob Dylan's 'Tambourine Man' with drums and biting twelve-string electric guitar. They did the same with Pete Seeger's 'Turn,

Turn, Turn'. It wasn't long before country music held a fascination for all kinds of musical artists who dabbled with the form, visited Nashville and eventually formed the phenomenally successful country rock boom of the 70s.

Bob Dylan's role in opening the rock world's eyes to country music is vital. He had a long-standing friendship with Johnny Cash and in 1966 Dylan went to Nashville to record. Initially the contradictions seemed enormous. Dylan, the bohemian voice of drug-oriented protest youth of America, in Nashville, home of reactionary values. But

Above, The album *Sweetheart of the Rodeo* by the Byrds was one of the first rock albums to lean heavily on country music and gave its name to the current stars, Sweethearts of the Rodeo.

Above and right, Roy Clarke,
an instrumental wizard, hit-
maker and host of Hee Haw,
met President and Mrs Carter.

Dylan's visit and his eventual *Nashville Skyline* album were successful musically and helped bring Nashville into the modern era.

On the west coast several groups sprang up who played authentic country music. A bluegrass outfit called The Dillards electrified young audiences, as did The Kentucky Colonels (with guitarist Clarence White, later to join The Byrds) and Country Gazette, which featured the outstanding fiddle skills of Byron Berline. But it was Gram Parsons who really fused together the elements – young audiences, rock music and country – with any real success. Berline recalls: 'There were a lot of people playing around with country on the west coast in the 60s but Gram kind of gets the credit because he surfaced. It wasn't that he was the best – I don't think he was – but he had a drive and a charisma that drew a focus towards him. He was a crazy mixed-up rich kid, but boy did he love country music.'

If country rock flourished in the 70s, then Parsons laid down the foundations with several musical permutations in the late 60s. His first combo, The International Sub-

marine Band, produced one shaky album before Parsons teamed up with The Byrds. Chris Hillman had an affinity with both folk and country, and with Parsons' obsessive drive The Byrds recorded more and more country material. Although many of Parsons' vocals were lost in the final mix of the album *Sweetheart Of The Rodeo*, his influence and songs were crucial to the band's new musical direction. In 1968 The Byrds were invited on stage at the Grand Ole Opry to perform Parsons' 'Hickory Wind'. The reception was lukewarm, but it was hardly surprising as they looked so different from the other performers.

Parsons left The Byrds in 1968 when he refused to tour South Africa, but the following year he came up with a new band (with Hillman alongside him), The Flying Burrito Brothers, probably the first and finest of all the country rock bands. Their début album, *The Gilded Palace Of Sin*, sounded very country but the sleeve image was hippy in tone, with marijuana leaves embroidered into their nudie suits. This certainly wasn't the country music of Chet Atkins and the Nashville Sound, but there was no doubt

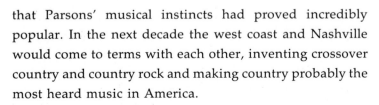

Above, Johnny Cash changed
the face of country. His work
with Bob Dylan attracted
attention from the rock world.

Left, Johnny Cash conducts his
affairs from the House of Cash,
a tourist attraction outside
Nashville, which is run by
family members.

that Parsons' musical instincts had proved incredibly
popular. In the next decade the west coast and Nashville
would come to terms with each other, inventing crossover
country and country rock and making country probably the
most heard music in America.

3
Country
Crossover

The 70s would be a boom period for country music. Never before had there been so much cross-fertilization, experimentation and creativity, and of course controversy as the question of what is and what is not country became an important topic of debate. Two broad areas developed, country rock and country pop, and a host of artists emerged as new superstars.

While it was Atkins and Owen Bradley who had pioneered country music's association with pop, it was another producer, Billy Sherrill, who finished the job almost singlehandedly by creating and defining a new country pop sound in the 70s. Sherrill made his name in Nashville in the 60s producing hits for Tammy Wynette and David Houston. While Atkins had misgivings about country moving too far away from its roots, Sherrill worked happily in the middle-of-the-road format. His liking was for hit singles rather than albums, being well aware that a

Previous page, centre, Kenny Rogers on the set of the television show, *Kenny Rogers and the American Cowboys*. Rogers has pursued his successful career through television, film and photography books.

Previous page, top, Willie Nelson, complete with bandanna and beard, the symbols of his latter-day style. As part of The Highwaymen, alongside Kristofferson, Waylon Jennings and Cash, he is still as popular as ever.

Above, Charley Rich in a tender moment with his wife. Essentially a jazz musician, Rich found great success with MOR country in the 70s.

smash single would generate healthy album sales. He wanted every single to sound different, to be sympathetic with the artist and to appeal to as broad a cross-section of listeners as possible. And although Sherrill caused controversy by ridding himself of traditional country instrumentation, he stuck with solidly country songs. Their lyric content was as before, the highly charged emotional delivery perfectly in tune with old-time music, but the execution was different. For some artists the new method worked exceptionally well, but others lost their biting edge and settled into semi-retirement. With Sherrill at the helm, Nashville was ready to become Nash Vegas.

Sherrill's most startling success came with Charlie Rich. By the mid 70s Rich was the highest-paid entertainer in country music. He ruled the country pop airwaves and sold records by the bucketload, but it was Sherrill's golden touch that made it possible. Rich was no new starlet, for by the time of his success he had already spent some twenty years as a musician and performer, at one time producing rock and roll at Sun before teaming up with Sherrill in the late 60s. Superstardom arrived with 'Behind Closed Doors', the epitome of the Sherrill sound. The song was a simple country ballad, the execution lush and sweet. The orchestrations were elaborate, set against a wall of overdubbed backing vocals. The song sold three million copies, its follow-up, 'The Most Beautiful Girl', two million and the next, 'A Very Special Love Song', one million. Charlie Rich had no barriers, and he expanded the horizons of the country star by appearing at Las Vegas and picking up numerous music awards. Rich's greying hair and smooth approach gave him the ideal image to break into the easygoing pop market. Here image was vital and for country artists to succeed fully in pop they needed something more than good songs and talent.

Tammy Wynette, another Sherrill artist, possessed a very strong and clear image. She was the modern woman who retained traditional values. She would assert herself but ultimately stand by her man. As a performer Wynette had magnetic stage presence and she became a voice for women in America. The George Jones and Wynette duet albums produced by Sherrill were inspired recordings. A real-life husband and wife singing of their love and fears was highly marketable, and if Sherrill understood anything it was the selling of a record and an idea. For some, Sherrill's over-elaborate arrangements hid Wynette's immense vocal talent, but they had tapped into a new market, one they defined as 'the middle-aged middle-class housewife who sympathized with the powerful sentiments of "Stand By Your Man" '.

Often accused of being a svengali figure, a manipulator of singers, Sherrill had his chance to create and package the image of a young girl, Tanya Tucker. With Rich and Wynette, Sherrill was working with seasoned performers who had already had some measure of success. With Tucker he was responsible for defining and honing a look and a sound. Sherrill discovered Tucker when she was just thirteen years old in 1972. He loved the power and innocence of her voice, but she had already had several years of experience with country music, having attended numerous concerts in Arizona with her star-struck father. He took her

Above, Ronnie Milsap put his blindness behind him, started out as a rocker and turned himself into a country star with a string of hits in the 70s and a couple of Grammy awards.

Above, Lacy J. Dalton has enjoyed mixed fortunes since Billy Sherill discovered her in the late 70s, and produced her début album. Still a Nashville mainstay, she has come a long way from her role as singer with the 60s acid rock group, Office.

Top and opposite, Tanya Tucker has been a star since she was 13. Moulded by hit-maker Billy Sherill, she made the transition from child to adult star with ease. In 1991 she won the female vocalist of the year award from the CMA on the same day as giving birth in a Nashville hospital.

to Nashville first when she was just nine years old, and not surprisingly they left empty-handed, but she did win a small part in the cult western movie *Jeremiah Johnson*. Her parents paid for her to record a demo tape, which is what Sherrill heard, and he immediately signed her. Once Sherrill had the right song, Tucker would explode. The song was 'Delta Dawn' and it went into the top ten. She followed that with 'Blood Red And Goin' Down' and 'Would You Lay With Me (In A Field Of Stone)'. It is easy to accuse Sherrill of packaging and manipulating the young star, but that notion detracts from Tucker's obvious talent. That she is still going strong after many turbulent episodes perhaps suggests that Sherrill was more a supporter than a svengali. In any case, her image was a breath of fresh air to country pop. She was young and so appealed to a new younger audience as well as to the traditional male mid-west market thanks to her overt sexuality on stage.

What Sherrill brought to country was a healthy respect for studio technology. Too often country records had been poorly produced, churned out by the same tired studio musicians who were competent but not as shimmering and

Right, John Denver sold
millions of records in the
country vein after starting out
as a folksinger in the 60s. His
'Take Me Home Country
Roads' has become a standard
for countless country bands.

Below, Kris Kristofferson with
his wife at the time, Rita
Coolidge. Coolidge was an
artist in her own right, though
her career slipped away with
the 70s.

clean as their pop cousins. Once Sherrill showed the way,
the doors opened for hi-tech country, and a host of
non-country performers felt able to adapt their pop style to
the Nashville environment.

Anne Murray topped the country charts in 1970 with
'Snowbird'. She was not a country performer. She was
Canadian and did not regard herself as country, but the
song sounded country and proved a smash. From 1970 to
1978 she had some twenty hits in the country charts before
going to greater heights in the late 70s with songs like
'Daydream Believer' and 'You Needed Me'. It was a testi-
mony to the new approach of country radio that Murray
was grabbed as a country artist.

Much the same happened for John Denver. He may have
been raised in the mountains but he made his name as a
folk singer before becoming the Country Music Association's Entertainer of the Year in 1975. While Denver had
been around for some time, writing 'Leaving On A Jet
Plane' for Peter, Paul and Mary and performing with folk
act The Chad Mitchell Trio, it wasn't until 'Take Me Home
Country Roads' that he became a genuine superstar.
Denver never claimed to be a country singer, did not
record in Nashville and never appeared on the Opry, but
still his records were played consistently on country radio
stations. Denver utilized up-to-the-minute technology in

the studio and on his live shows. Lyrically his songs had a nostalgic rural flavour and showed clearly that country music was becoming a much looser term than ever before. Country radio stations gladly played records by rock acts so long as the song sounded vaguely country. Consequently, by the mid 70s country radio airwaves were filled by artists such as The Eagles, Paul McCartney, The Pointer Sisters, The Amazing Rhythm Aces and a bright young Australian singer, Olivia Newton John.

The case around Newton John and the debate as to whether she was country or not is a perfect illustration of the dilemma country music and Nashville was in by the mid 70s. Olivia Newton John surfaced in Britain as a pop singer but in America her records got the most plays on country radio. However, she upset the Nashville establishment, and fifty of Nashville's older stars met at George Jones' home and organised a protest, ostensibly to complain about the lack of traditional country artists on the Country Music Association board but in fact to fight back at the growing number of pop artists infiltrating the country charts and country radio. But Nashville and the industry establishment was riding high financially, pop crossover had led to a massive boom in recording in Nashville, and sales of country records were at their highest point. And if the older artists felt threatened and neglected, a group of younger musicians opted to fight back. They were anti-Nashville, anti-country pop, anti-Billy Sherrill, but very much pro-country music. These were the Outlaws.

A media term, the Outlaw movement really revolved around three artists, Kris Kristofferson, Willie Nelson and Waylon Jennings. They disliked the softening of country music and set about creating country with roots. In the process they changed the face of 70s country music and made it even more popular with rock audiences than the pop country artists had done. Initially, however, there was a good deal of antipathy between the rebels and Nashville. Kris Kristofferson, from Texas and a Rhodes scholar, started writing country tunes as Kris Carson in the 60s. He moved to Nashville in 1966, recorded demos and worked at numerous menial jobs (he was once a janitor at Johnny Cash's studio). His early songs were straightforward simple country and were recorded by the likes of Faron Young, Roy Drusky and Bobby Bare. But soon Kristofferson was easing himself into a group of young writers who lived outside the Nashville norm. Writers like Mickey Newbury and Tony Joe White were more concerned with creativity and art than they were with making money. They had long

Above, Willie Nelson moved out of Nashville to become an Outlaw in Texas. He starred in movies, sold millions of records, established Farm Aid and ran into trouble with the IRS, to whom he owed over $17 million. Despite the setbacks he remains a major star.

Above, Ronnie Milsap accepts a gold disc award. His friend Waylon Jennings has clearly enjoyed the RCA records reception.

Top, Waylon Jennings and Jessi Colter, with Jack Clement – songwriter, record producer, part-time singer, musician, raconteur and one of Nashville's most colourful characters.

hair and fitted the hippy image more than the southern redneck. As Kristofferson says, 'To us, being commercial was a dirty word. Nashville had gotten very clean-cut – I guess we felt closer to the spirit of Hank Williams.'

When Dylan recorded *Nashville Skyline* in Nashville, Kristofferson felt his view that country was a serious art form had been endorsed. Kristofferson let his songwriting wander and 'Me and Bobby McGee', as recorded by Roger Miller, was a massive hit in 1969. Johnny Cash recorded 'Sunday Morning Coming Down', which won the CMA song of the year award in 1970. Kristofferson had further success with 'Help Me Make It Through The Night' but then left country music for Hollywood. He was not the most commercially successful of the rebels, but his frank songwriting, his rebel image and love of a simple country song inspired others who would further challenge the Nashville status quo.

Willie Nelson, who had been in Nashville for some time before Kristofferson arrived, had some success as a writer penning the Patsy Cline classic 'Crazy' and Faron Young's 'Hello Walls'. His own recordings, however, did not fare so well. When Kristofferson broke through, Nelson's own freewheeling spirit, which had been held in check in Nashville, was released. He started hanging out with the long-haired nonconformists. In 1971 his house in Nashville burned down and Nelson moved back to Texas. It would rapidly change his career.

Texas had always played an important part in Nelson's musical heritage. He formed a new base in Austin, let his hair and beard grow, signed with Atlantic in New York and recorded 'Shotgun Willie'. He used non-Nashville players, including Doug Sahm and ex-Bob Wills fiddle player Johnny Gimble, and finally found the style and voice that allowed his songwriting and singing to flourish. He started playing concerts in Texas and organized a festival in Dripping, Texas, which put his favourite artists, the old and the new, on one bill. He had the new wave – Kristofferson, Tom T. Hall and Waylon Jennings – alongside old Nashville stalwarts Bill Monroe and Roy Acuff. In 1975 Nelson recorded *Red-Headed Stranger*, an album of simple music and beautiful lyrics. The record company wanted strings but Nelson stood firm and the only strings heard were from his characteristic nylon-strung guitar.

Waylon Jennings surfaced alongside Nelson as the archetypal Outlaw star. He too had been a Nashville artist, leaning on a folky sound in the 60s, and had a handful of hits with songs like 'Walk On Out Of My Mind' (1968) and 'Only Daddy That'll Walk The Line' (1968). By the 70s he

Opposite, Willie Nelson.
Dogged by tax problems these
days, Nelson has had a long
and varied career, from
songsmithing to superstar
and movie actor.

Above, Waylon Jennings and
Jessi Colter rivalled George
Jones and Tammy Wynette as
country music's favourite
married team in the 70s.
Jennings was a rebel long
before he became an Outlaw.

Left and opposite, Tompall
Glaser was a key figure behind
the Outlaw movement. His
business dealings enabled
the new breed of artists to
do things their own way.
Together with his brothers,
Chuck and Jim, Tompall was
also a formidable artist in
his own right.

was fighting the Nashville system. He picked material
from the new young writers and fought to win himself an
independent production deal.

In 1976 RCA released an album that made country music
history. *Wanted The Outlaws*, featuring Waylon Jennings,
Willie Nelson, Tompall Glaser and Jessi Colter, sold over a
million copies. The music was a return to the road-house
sound and it sold the image of the Outlaw to the whole of
America. Country music was again going back to its roots.

Tompall Glaser was a key artist in the Outlaw movement
but his significance rests with his considerable business
acumen. He had a successful song publishing business and
used the profits to build a recording studio that could be
utilized by the new breed of country artist. While Willie
and Waylon grabbed the headlines, Tompall was there
behind them, and Nelson and Jennings went from success
to success with top-selling albums, singles and concerts
throughout the 70s.

David Allan Coe fitted the Outlaw mould with ease. Before coming to Nashville in 1967 he had spent some twenty years in reform schools and prisons. He quickly learned the importance of image and, as the Mysterious Rhinestone Cowboy, travelled around Nashville in a hearse. David Allan Coe arrived as a country artist, initially as the writer of smash hits like 'Would You Lay With Me (In A Field Of Stone)' for Tanya Tucker, but he went on to be a steady album-seller, even cutting an album entitled *Waylon, Willie and Me*.

The Outlaw trend was significant in itself but had some far-reaching effects. By moving out of Nashville it brought the music of Texas back into the public eye, it inspired a wave of southern rock bands and, most significantly, stopped Nashville taking country down a pop cul-de-sac. Jennings recorded a song in 1975, 'Bob Wills Is Still The King', that made specific references to the differences between Nashville and Texas. At the same time there

Opposite, David Allen Coe was one of the more colourful figures of the 70s. Too wild to be an Outlaw, he allegedly killed a man in prison. His often crude lyrics upset Nashville, but he made a name for himself as a writer for Tanya Tucker. Seen here with punks (top) on the Kings Road, London.

Below and right, Asleep At The Wheel have been around since the mid 70s. An ever-changing line-up (in which mainstay Ray Benson has been the only original member to remain with the band) has kept the music fresh, and ensured lasting popularity for their swinging concerts and their brand of Texas swing.

began a revival in western swing music led by Asleep At The Wheel and Alvin Crow And The Pleasant Valley Boys. Both bands played traditional Bob Wills style but with a slight rock undertone. A Californian band, Commander Cody and The Lost Planet Airmen, fused swing with rock, soul and country and had success with rock audiences. The year that Commander Cody broke up, 1976, saw the forma-tion of another Texas band, ZZ Top, now a major rock band but then a group trying out all kinds of Texas music.

If the Outlaws gave country back its bite, then the southern rock bands gave country a hefty kick. The early 70s country rock bands from California softened their music with country harmonies. The southern country rock bands, first and foremost country outfits, added rock to their bar-room sound and scored several triumphs. The Charlie Daniels Band was perhaps the perfect example of southern country rock. While other southern bands such as Marshall Tucker and The Allman Brothers had roots in country, Daniels was the most country of them all. Their music was raw, abandoned and frenetic, with Daniels himself at the fore. He modernized such classics as 'Orange Blossom Special' and 'Fire In The Mountain' and had an international hit with 'Devil Went Down To Georgia'.

Hank Williams Jr, the son of the country music legend, had enjoyed straight country hits since 1964 (when he was in his mid teens) but did not succeed in casting off the shadow of his famous father until he changed his style to southern country rock. His breakthrough album in 1975, *Hank Williams Jr and Friends*, had featured guest musicians from several southern rock bands, and he looked all set for

Previous page, far left, Hank Williams Jr. His life and career have been as troubled as his father's; but Hank Jr has found a niche for himself as country music's wild man, famed for his roaring rock shows.

Previous page, Charlie Daniels with his band in London (bottom) and roping steers on his ranch (top).

Below, Alabama enjoyed unrivalled success in the late 70s and 80s. Their soft rock-meets-country sound appealed to both country and rock fans.

superstardom when disaster struck and he had a near-fatal accident, falling down a Montana mountainside. He made a remarkable recovery and two years later re-emerged to make a string of increasingly successful albums. A hell-raiser by nature, Hank Jr is now one of the biggest names in contemporary country.

A country supergroup of the 70s, Alabama, played a gentler country rock and had phenomenal success. Alabama took the close harmony style of the California country rock outfits and spiced it up with a down-home Dixie sound and became for a while the biggest-selling group in country music history.

Right, Chris Hillman's Desert Rose Band brought Hillman back to country music after working with the Byrds in the 60s. Alongside excellent musicians, John Jorgenson (left) and Herb Pedersen (centre), he made some of the most graceful country music of the late 80s.

Above, Charlie Daniels meets President and Mrs Carter.

The bluegrass revival of the 70s came from the same desire to take country back to its roots as the Outlaw movement. It also brought old-time performers together with new artists as Willie Nelson had done with his early 70s concerts. The Opry had some performers, notably bluegrass maestro Bill Monroe, Jim and Jesse and The Osborne Brothers, but the music had a strong grass-roots following across the States, even in the North where it appealed to the urban folk crowd. A bluegrass festival circuit grew up where performers played several shows and stayed around the site to give workshops and advice to would-be performers.

Flatt and Scruggs, both one-time members of Monroe's Bluegrass Boys band, made bluegrass nationally known in the 60s with their music for the TV show The Beverly Hillbillies. The Hollywood movie *Deliverance* created a hit with old-time 'Dueling Banjos'. College kids like Bill Keith and Peter Rowan sought out Monroe and learned everything they could from him before bringing their own talents to the form. Earl Scruggs was happy to play with the younger musicians, many of whom appeared out of Washington DC, and he brought his phenomenal banjo-playing to numerous country rock albums. The youngsters played rock tunes bluegrass style and came up with the term newgrass, of which the Newgrass Revival were the most successful exponents, while The Seldom Scene, The Country Gentlemen, J. D. Crowe and The New South kept old-time instruments alive but in a modern format.

Above, Music publisher Wesley Rose with (left to right) Mickey Newbury, Emmylou Harris and Don Everly. Rose praised Harris for her dedication towards traditional country music.

Opposite, Emmylou Harris, who came from Birmingham, Alabama, only became involved in country after attempting to pursue a career in folk music. She even wrote to Pete Seeger, the folk guru, for advice. Her work with Gram Parsons launched her country career, and since the 70s she has been a mainstay of acoustic-based country music.

Country music in the 70s was now a very broad church. Indeed, even the rock world became involved in country. In the country rock field Emmylou Harris, still a power-house in the 90s, had a direct link with Gram Parsons and the fledgling country rock experiment. She met Parsons in Washington DC and was soon on the west coast adding harmonies to his mournful ballads and up tempo rockers. Before that she had been yet another folkie wandering around the Washington DC coffee houses armed with a jumbo acoustic guitar. She had even written to folk guru Pete Seeger asking for help and advice. Emmylou was a single parent but she was determined to make it in the music business. She recalls: 'I had a drive. I wanted to sing. My parents were really supportive and helped me, particularly with my daughter.' As in most country success stories, fate smiled sweetly on the struggling chanteuse. Parsons whisked her away to a new career with country. As she remembers, 'Working with Gram was a wonderful experience. He was wildly misunderstood, too country for the rockers and too weird for the Nashville establishment. But he had a vision and a real love for those old mountain harmonies. I learned more than I can tell from Gram.'

When Parsons died Emmylou devoted her early career to creating the kind of sound Parsons was always searching for. 'The idea was always to keep the country pure, to keep the instruments country but give it a rock kick. That's why there's a big difference between what they call country rock and country pop. With country pop the authenticity and purity of country music was lost, hidden behind string and background choirs. I mean some of the songs were wonderful but I didn't really care for the overall style.' Her début album *Pieces Of The Sky* won great critical and public acclaim. She has maintained an uncompromising stance with her music, seeing off trends and fads and eventually witnessing country coming back to its traditional roots in the early 80s.

Linda Ronstadt emerged in the 70s as one of the leading exponents of country rock. Never as pure country sounding as Emmylou Harris, she adapted the carefree west coast country style to a rock backing and found incredible success. She started out in Los Angeles as a folkie, hanging out at hootenannies at The Troubador alongside other hopefuls like Stephen Stills, Neil Young and Roger McGuinn. She joined a folk rock outfit, The Stone Poneys, and recorded Mike Nesmith's 'Different Drum'. It was a hit in 1967 and Ronstadt was on her way. Her early albums were essentially rock-orientated but there was no disguising the country influences. She recorded her first solo album, *Silk Purse*, in Nashville with Nashville musicians, and for her *Linda Ronstadt* album in 1970 she put together a band featuring Glenn Frey, Don Henley and Randy Meisner, all of whom would eventually form The Eagles, the most commercially successful country rock band of them all. Ronstadt is not a writer but as an interpreter of songs she has few equals. Her penchant for country saw her record several songs by country legends, notably Hank Williams' 'I Can't Help It (If I'm Still In Love With You)' and Phil Everly's 'When Will I Be Loved'. Slowly she moved away from country to a more solidly rock format but came back to the genre in the 80s with the award-winning *Trio* album alongside Dolly Parton and Emmylou Harris which saw the three women blending incredible harmonies on straight-down-the-line country material.

The New Riders Of The Purple Sage also gave rock fans a taste of country. The band grew out of The Grateful Dead (whose *Workingman's Dead* had a strong country flavour) and featured Jerry Garcia on pedal steel. The line-up and output of the band fluctuated and changed over the years until they called it quits in the mid 70s. At their best The New Riders worked hard at fusing country with rock.

Opposite, Linda Ronstadt, the brightest face of country rock, had her first hit with 'Different Drum', a country-like tune written by Mike Nesmith of the Monkees. In the 70s her smooth, laid-back style epitomized California country.

Above, Dolly Parton, Linda Ronstadt and Emmylou Harris found time in their busy schedules to record an innovative acoustic album, *Trio*, in 1987.

While Commander Cody And The Lost Planet Airmen played a somewhat crazed style of country rock, The Pure Prairie League took a softer approach as did Poco, who developed into one of the biggest-selling soft rock bands of the late 70s. Before they broke through to pop success in 1976 with 'Crazy Love', Poco had been recording critically acclaimed country rock albums for nearly ten years. Formed by Jim Meisner and Richey Furey of Buffalo Springfield fame, for a while at least they produced some of the most graceful fusions of country and rock and roll music.

Michael Nesmith is also closely associated with the pioneering of this new country sound. As a Monkee he had pushed his Texas twang high into the mix and recorded several country songs with the group before going solo with his classic country rock albums in the early 70s which, while never selling millions, certainly showed the way artistically. Some of his songs like 'Propinquity' and 'Some Of Shelly's Blues' were recorded by Linda Ronstadt and The Nitty Gritty Dirt Band.

The Nitty Gritty Dirt Band, still going strong in mainstream contemporary country, began back in the mid 60s as a jig-band-meets-rock-meets-folk-meets-country concept. Jackson Browne was a member of the group in its early days, and they soon had a hit with 'Mr Bojangles'. Their importance in the 70s, however, came with the dramatic *Will The Circle Be Unbroken* album which saw the new country players record with the old. The Dirt Band's banjo player, John McEuen, was the driving force behind the project. He had long been a fan of banjo legend Earl Scruggs and one night, after attending a Scruggs appearance in Colorado, dared to suggest that the banjo legend do some work with the Dirt Band. Scruggs was surprisingly enthusiastic. The eventual line-up made the recording session one of the most important in Nashville history. Scruggs, Maybelle Carter, Vassar Clements, Merle Travis, Doc Watson and Roy Acuff teamed up with a bunch of long-haired hippy types calling themselves The Nitty Gritty Dirt Band. Says McEuen: 'We just wanted to give those older musicians credit for what they'd done. It was a real honour to play with them. We wanted the kids who liked country rock to see where it all came from.'

But it was The Eagles from California who took country rock to its pinnacle. Don Henley, Randy Meisner, Glenn Frey and Bernie Leadon sold millions of records with their characteristic free-flowing, harmony-heavy country sound. Their first two albums, *Eagles* and *Desperado*, were seminal country rock pieces. When *Hotel California* went gold in 1976 it was their sixth album to do so, and while they moved towards country rock when guitarist Joe Walsh joined, they probably defined the term country rock better than anybody in the 70s.

While the west coast country flirtation certainly made the sound of fiddles and mountain harmonies palatable to a rock audience, they had little impact on Nashville. Chet Atkins recalls: 'We were aware of what was going on but their music came foremost from rock, whereas the kind of changes we were making were firmly rooted in country music.'

Opposite, The Nitty Gritty Dirt Band has stunned both country and rock audiences with their blend of the two styles since the late 60s. Their seminal album, *Will The Circle Be Unbroken*, brought old-timers like Roy Acuff into the same studio as long-haired youngsters from the Dirt Band.

Above, Joe Ely from Texas played a rough brand of country rock in the 70s. Adopted by British punk band, The Clash, he opened several shows for them. A leading light in the Texas music scene, his recording career has yet to reflect his true talent.

Country music had survived controversy and stylistic revolutions and no matter what the media or artists called the new styles, country music was still country music. Throughout the changes some artists continued to sing with a country voice, while others managed to adapt their sound to whatever was happening at the time. Dolly Parton fits into both these categories. On the one hand she became an entertainment superstar by reaching a huge crossover market and relocating to Los Angeles; on the other hand, she continued to perform straight-down-the-line country music.

Parton's life and career really does read like a Horatio Alger novel. The epitome of the rags to riches story, she came from a dirt-poor mountain family in Tennessee. Her family used music as rural folk had done for so many years – it was entertainment and a buffer against the hard times. With an obvious musical talent, Dolly began to look at music as a way out of poverty. 'None of my family had ever left the mountains. But I, as far back as I remember, had this urge to see what else there was. And it was music that made that possible for me.' As a child she sang in public as often as she could, and right after leaving high school in 1964 she moved to Nashville, finding some success with a song ironically entitled 'Dumb Blonde'. She joined the Porter Wagoner show, singing straight country and doing several duets with Wagoner. By 1974 she felt frustrated and went on her own. She received numerous awards for her songwriting, and won the top female country singer awards from the CMA in 1975 and 1976. Her appearance at the 1976 Grammy awards caused a riotous ovation.

Parton clearly had star quality, something television quickly realized by giving her a syndicated show in the mid 70s. She had enormous record success in the 70s with hits like 'Love Is Like A Butterfly', 'The Bargain Store', 'Coat Of Many Colors' and 'Jolene'. She eventually moved into movies and is now very much a Hollywood superstar. But while other crossover acts tended to leave their country roots behind, Parton never did. 'I may have left Nashville but I still love country music. I have never forgotten where

Right, Dolly Parton. Not content with successful careers in music, television and films, Dolly started a theme park, Dollywood, high in the Smokey Mountains of Tennessee. The park offers both a museum to her past and a source of work for the small community she left behind.

Right, Dolly Parton. Although the first hit to set her on her way was entitled 'Dumb Blonde', Parton has been anything but dumb and has proved one of the most successful crossover country stars of all time.

Opposite, top, Barbara Mandrell (centre) with sisters Louise (left) and Irlene. Barbara Mandrell is one of country pop's most successful artists. A natural entertainer, Barbara and her sisters had a popular television show in the 80s.

Opposite, bottom, Barbara Mandrell created a connection between country music and tourism with her museum and gift store.

I came from and I go back all the time' (she built a massive theme park near her home, Dollywood). 'I don't think my songs have lost their country sound. Some things are very pop, but I'll do real mountain country as well. I can't see what's wrong with doing different things and having your songs heard by as many people as possible. I've never really fitted in anyway. My voice was unusual right from the start. It kinda wanders around, you know, and I guess the way I dress and look is a little unusual too. But that's all part of where I come from too. We really did have nothing when I was a kid so as soon as I had the money I went way over the top.'

Barbara Mandrell came close to rivalling Parton's dramatic across-the-board success but never quite became an international superstar. Like Parton she made her name with glitzy frocks and a Vegas showbiz persona, but she had very credible credits as a musician before hitting the stardom trail. She started as a member of the Mandrell's family band and toured overseas in the mid 60s with the Johnny Cash show. She already had an eye on the growing country pop world when she moved to Nashville in the late 60s and teamed up with producer Billy Sherrill. Her first attempts at recordings were country versions of soul hits, but it was not until 'Standing Room Only' and a follow-up string of ballads in the mid 70s that she really came of age as a Nashville star. From 1980 to 1982 she had her own NBC television series in which, along with her sisters, Louise and Irlene, she showcased her dexterous musical and instrumental skills. Louise also made quite a name for herself in the mid 80s.

Right, Crystal Gayle, the younger sister of Loretta Lynn, started singing on her sister's shows before becoming a star in her own right with hits such as 'Don't It Make My Brown Eyes Blue'. She is reputed to have the longest hair in the business.

Opposite, Kenny Rogers picked up a whole host of awards in the 70s. His easy-going manner appealed to country and pop fans alike. He has worked for his success, however. His first record, a jazz album in 1966, sank without trace.

Below, Texas has consistently provided country music with some of its more colourful characters.

Crystal Gale had enormous country pop success from 1975 to 1986. The younger sister of Loretta Lynn, she started touring with her sister before going solo in the early 70s. Once she teamed up with producer Allen Reynolds it was success all the way, with international hits such as 'Don't It Make Your Brown Eyes Blue' and 'Talkin' In Your Sleep'.

However successful all these artists were in the crossover field, none could match the phenomenal profile of Kenny Rogers. Rogers played several kinds of music, including pop, jazz and folk, before giving country a shot in the mid 70s. His first Nashville single, 'Love Lifted Me', did pretty well but it was 'Lucille' in 1977 that made Rogers a worldwide success. More than any other, Rogers managed to switch from real country with songs like 'The Gambler' to mainstream pop with consummate ease. Like Parton, Rogers moved away from the restrictions of Nashville by putting himself into the mainstream eye. He appeared on several network entertainment television shows and collected country music and Grammy awards. As he entered the next decade he recorded more pop hits and scored a massive international hit with a duet with Dolly Parton, 'Islands In The Sun'. To date he has made more than ten television specials and five television movies and mini series, including the very popular Gambler series. And just to prove he is a man of many parts, Rogers has also published two books of his photography.

URBAN COWBOY
ORIGINAL MOTION PICTURE SOUNDTRACK

JIMMY BUFFETT

CHARLIE DANIELS BAND

EAGLES

DAN FOGELBERG

MICKEY GILLEY

GILLEY'S
"URBAN COWBOY" BAND

JOHNNY LEE

ANNE MURRAY

BONNIE RAITT

LINDA RONSTADT/
J. D. SOUTHER

KENNY ROGERS

BOZ SCAGGS

BOB SEGER AND
THE SILVER BULLET BAND

JOE WALSH

4
New
Country

T he 1980s opened with a country music bang. Out in
Hollywood John Travolta was cast in a movie that
was designed to tap into the music movie genre that had
made *Saturday Night Fever* a phenomenal success. Instead
of the disco, *Urban Cowboy* focused on the modern-day
cowboy scene. And while the movie may not have gar-
nered Travolta any awards or critical accolades, it pushed
the cowboy image and country music to the media fore and
for a while trend-setters across the States played country
and dressed in blue jeans, hats and cowboy boots. Suddenly country music was a fashion accessory and Nashville
was sufficiently established to make the most of its tem-
porary national attention.

Set in the Texas honky-tonk scene, the movie had a
blistering country soundtrack featuring artists like Charlie
Daniels, Anne Murray and Bonnie Roitt. And for two
country acts, Mickey Gilley and Johnny Lee, the movie

Previous page, centre, The cowboy image has shaped country music since the days of the singing cowboys, with the stetson forming as essential an ingredient as the guitar. Artists like Michael Martin Murphey have made a career from recreating the wild west life-style in music.

Previous page, top, *Urban Cowboy*, with a biting country and country rock soundtrack, made country music very fashionable across America.

Right, Johnny Lee (left) and his cousin Mickey Gilley at Gilley's in Pasadena, Texas, the club featured in the film, *Urban Cowboy*.

Opposite, Country music has fared well on the big screen, from records of performances, such as *Country Music*, to Clint Eastwood comedies like *Every Which Way But Loose*. Marty Robbins, an "all-round" entertainer once commented that "music was better than working for a living".

Above, Burt Reynolds and Jerry Reed at the CMA awards show. Reynolds himself is a considerable country fan and dated Tammy Wynette in the 70s. He and Reed collaborated on the successful *Smokey and the Bandit* films.

changed their careers overnight. Much of the movie was filmed in Gilley's club, Gilley's in Pasadena. A cousin of Jerry Lee Lewis and Jimmy Swaggart, he had been recording for several years and had a number one on Playboy Records with 'Roomful Of Roses' in 1974. His role in *Urban Cowboy* proved a great career boost and established Gilley as a household name. Johnny Lee also benefited from *Urban Cowboy*. He had several small hits from his Texas base and was a good friend of Gilley's prior to the movie. They duetted in the film on 'Mamas Don't Let Your Babies Grow Up To Be Cowboys', but it was Lee's own 'Lookin' For Love' that gave him a million-selling hit single.

Urban Cowboy was not the first time Hollywood had dabbled with country music. It had started of course with the Singing Cowboys and country had provided a scenario for several low-budget B movies in the 50s and 60s (*Hillbillies In A Haunted House* and *Cotton Pickin' Chicken Pickers* being two of the more snappy titles). But as country music became more respectable, Hollywood's treatment of it improved. Robert Altman's *Nashville* from 1975 dealt with a grander social overview than just music, but it did treat the music town seriously. Kris Kristofferson moved from a country singing and writing career to big-time movies, none of which had real country roots, but two established Hollywood stars allowed their affection for the country lifestyle and music to infiltrate their movies. Burt Reynolds, who had made an album in Nashville in 1973, took the lead with a 1975 movie, *WW And The Dixie Dance Kings*, a low-key film that focused on road life for a touring country band. Aside from Reynolds, the movie featured a young Don Williams, Jerry Reed and Connie Van Dyke from the country music world.

Then came Clint Eastwood with the commercially successful *Every Which Way But Loose* in 1978 and its follow-up *Any Which Way You Can*, both of which spent plenty of film time in west coast honky-tonks and spawned popular country soundtracks. Eastwood again used a country soundtrack for *Bronco Billy* in 1980 and went all the way two years later with *Honky-Tonk Man*, in which he played a small-time country singer heading for an audition on the Grand Ole Opry in the 30s. The movie featured appear-ances from Johnny Gimble, Ray Price and Marty Robbins. Hardly a country movie, *Nine To Five* in 1980 saw Dolly Parton bringing her down-home persona to the silver screen, while *The Electric Horseman* in 1979 featured an appearance by Willie Nelson. Although *Urban Cowboy* was phenomenally successful as a movie and produced four million sales of the soundtrack album, it was *Coalminer's Daughter* that legitimately portrayed country people and country music in full-blown Hollywood fashion. *Coalminer's Daughter*, taken from the life-story of Loretta Lynn, was the second most popular movie in America in 1980. Moreover, Sissy Spacek won an Academy Award for her stunning portrayal of Loretta Lynn. A few years later Patsy Cline's story received a similar treatment in Karel Reisz's *Sweet Dreams*, with Jessica Lange playing the tempestuous country star.

When in Southern California visit Universal City Studios

Come along with
Marty Robbins
from the Heart of Nashville
to jumpin' Las Vegas!

"Country Music"
co-starring
SAMMY JACKSON with BARBARA MANDRELL • DOTTIE WEST • CARL SMITH
MARTY ROBBINS, JR. Produced and Directed by ROBERT HINKLE • A UNIVERSAL RELEASE
TECHNICOLOR® G GENERAL AUDIENCES All Ages Admitted

COPYRIGHT ©1972 BY UNIVERSAL PICTURES COUNTRY OF ORIGIN U.S.A.   LITHO. IN U.S.A.   5   72/334

Opposite, top, Rosanne Cash, Johnny's daughter, surprised Nashville with her unconventional image in the early 80s. Although she is now in New York and no longer a country musician, several of her albums, notably *Kings Record Shop*, are contemporary country classics.

Opposite, bottom, Lee Greenwood, a phenomenally big seller over the years, seems elated at getting off his own tour bus. This does not mean that the bus is cramped. On the contrary, Nashville stars travel in the ultimate comfort and luxury.

Right and below, Don Williams, the quiet man of country music. William's concerts have become renowned for their gentle laid-back style. As he says, 'I really don't like to make a big fuss on stage, just sing the songs. I think the audiences like it too.'

By the early 80s, then, country music had a very visible image. The music itself had crossed over into a slew of styles throughout the 70s and all of a sudden, thanks mainly to *Urban Cowboy*, the western look spread throughout cities in America. In a couple of years the dilution of country would create a backlash, but as the 80s turned, artists continued to sell records by the bucketload and not just to country fans.

Don Williams, the quietly spoken singer and writer from

Texas, had had hits in the country market since the early 70s (and gained pop success in the UK with 'I Recall A Gypsy Woman'), but in 1980 enjoyed a crossover smash 'I Believe In You'. While others looked for crossover success by moving from their country roots, adopting a more metropolitan look and softening their accents, Williams stuck to a simple, almost bare, instrumental style and found pop appeal without ever searching for it.

T. G. Sheppard, whose real name was Bill Browder, peaked in the early 80s. He had been around since the 60s and had a number one in 1974 with 'The Devil In The Bottle'. He had written the song himself but was unable to find an artist to record it, so he did it himself, coming up with the name T. G. Sheppard. He began a string of hits before crossing over with 'I Love 'Em Every One' in 1981. Janie Fricke found wide appeal around 1982 and 1983, having been discovered by hit-maker Billy Sherrill. He came across her as a backing singer and pushed her dulcet tones high in the mix on records by Crystal Gayle, Tanya Tucker and Ronnie Milsap. Finally she went solo and scored a trail of hits, starting with 'What You're Doing Tonight' in 1977. She was voted CMA female vocalist of the year in both 1982 and 1983. Sherrill did it again with Lacy J. Dalton, a raunchy rock-flavoured singer who turned straight country in the late 70s and had a major hit with a remake of Roy Orbison's 'Dream Baby' in 1983.

Crossover success came in a roundabout fashion for Sylvia. She moved to Nashville from Indiana and worked as a secretary before impressing at an audition with Dave and Sugar. She failed the audition but won a contract with RCA and had a massive pop country hit in 1983 with 'Nobody'. Indeed, country pop seemed to suit the talents of several female artists at this time. Charly McClain and Terri Gibbs both made inroads. Somewhat more rocky, Juice Newton had an international hit with 'Angel Of The Morning' in 1981 and Johnny Cash's daughter Rosanne kept the family name at the top of the charts with 'My Baby Thinks He's A Train' and 'Blue Moon With A Heartache'.

It was not just the women who enjoyed popular acclaim at this time. Lee Greenwood peaked in the early 80s. Yet another artist who had spent several years working his way to national attention, Greenwood got his first break as a jack of all styles performer in Las Vegas. By the early 80s he was ready for the new broad church in Nashville and a top twenty hit with 'It Turns Me Inside Out' in 1981. After that breakthrough the door to success was thrown open, hit followed hit and he won the CMA male vocalist award in 1983, quickly followed by a Grammy.

But the predominance of the pop sound in country music was not pleasing everyone in Nashville. The *Urban Cowboy* boom did send sales of country records through the roof, but only temporarily. Country pop had peaked and sales after that boom were levelling out. The country airwaves were ruled by a body of artists who had been around for some time. The record companies were not sure whether to stick with their stalwart artists, even if sales across the board were down, or to try something new. As in the past, it was the musicians themselves who pointed the way. The future meant looking backwards with the so-called new traditionalist movement. Both Ricky Skaggs and Emmylou Harris, who played key roles in the resurgence of old-time country sounds, felt that country had become too pop in the 80s. 'Some of it was so bland', commented Emmylou, 'that it sounded like elevator music to me.' Skaggs added: 'Listening to country radio at that time, there wasn't much to hear that had any real country roots.'

Skaggs played a significant musical contribution to Harris' seminal *Roses In The Snow* album in 1980. The album stood out at the time thanks to its use of old-time mountain

Above, The award-winning *Roses in the Snow* album from Emmylou Harris set the tone for the new traditionalist movement which subsequently took Nashville by storm in the mid 80s.

Opposite, Emmylou Harris may not enjoy the same popularity on radio country programmes that she once achieved, but she is still one of the most important figures in modern country music. Her last album was recorded at the legendary Ryman Auditorium.

Right, Ricky Skaggs is one of Nashville's most respected musicians and has in large part pioneered the new traditionalist sound, with its return to the basics.

Right, Sharon White and Ricky Skaggs. Skaggs had been a fan of Sharon since he heard her sing as a child with her family group, The Whites. They are now happily married.

Below and opposite, Reba McEntire is currently a key figure in country music. She outsells most other acts with RCA Records by a very considerable margin and runs her own affairs together with her husband and manager, Narvel Blackstock.

sounds. Within a year Skaggs was scoring his own hits and pioneering a new trend in country music. From Kentucky, Skaggs was an instrumental virtuoso as a child, playing in various bluegrass bands, including Ralph Stanley's outfit at just fifteen years of age. He moved through several bluegrass bands and eventually had his own, Boone Creek, before gaining wider attention as a member of Emmylou Harris' hot band. Epic Records gave him a chance as a solo act in 1981 and his début album *Waitin' For The Sun To Shine* went gold. Clearly his brand of mountain music, which had been marginalized in Nashville through the 70s, still had a part to play. Even so, the significance of the new traditionalist movement lay not just in the nostalgic re-creation of a lost sound but in the way it was done. As Skaggs recalls: 'What I had in mind was to bring back the old instruments, get rid of the synthesizer sound. But at the same time I wanted to use the recording technology used by contemporary musicians. Bit of old, bit of new and hopefully come up with something different.'

The establishment was quick to see that Skaggs was on to something and in 1982 he was voted CMA male vocalist of the year. When Skaggs had a number one hit with Bill Monroe's 'Uncle Pen', it was the first time that a bluegrass tune had topped the chart since 1949. His rise to prominence was meteoric and while others followed his brand of

new traditional country and some surpassed him in terms of media attention and record sales, Skaggs' significance in setting the ball rolling and giving Nashville a new integrity is second to none. These days he is something of an industry veteran, has produced an album for Dolly Parton, runs his own publishing company and still has hit records. But so great was Skaggs' impact in the mid 80s that a host of artists were quick to follow his musical path.

If Skaggs took the male lead, then Reba McEntire made a bold cry for women. Indeed, one of the features of contemporary country music is the abundance of female artists. McEntire is surely a role model to many. She was already an established artist when she announced to Billboard, 'We're going traditional country. No, I'll take that back . . . we want to do new country. We're wanting to go new Loretta Lynn, to get new pickers, young pickers who are

like me and want to stay country.' McEntire, from Oklahoma, joined a country band while still at school. Singing the national anthem at the National Rodeo Finals, she so impressed Red Steagall that he set her on her way to Nashville and a deal with Mercury. Her first album appeared in 1978 and already her style was evident. McEntire looked for drama, performed with unbridled passion and sang songs that placed women in a position of strength. Her move to MCA in 1984 coincided with the new traditionalist movement and all of a sudden her back to basics style made her a bona fide star. That year she won the CMA female vocalist award, and repeated the feat a year later, and again in 1986 and 1987.

McEntire's career has continued to grow and she is probably the most consistently popular female artist in contemporary country music. Even in the video age she is

very aware that a country artist has to put in a large chunk of road-work in order to see sales results. 'When I was off the road for about five months after I had my baby, my record sales and radio plays slumped. I've been around a long time but this business, especially in the 90s, is so competitive that you have to be continually working.' Not content with music, McEntire has diversified into movies and television. She had a part in the sci-fi film *Tremors* and a role in the television movie *The Gambler Returns* along-side Kenny Rogers. Her acting abilities have ensured that her videos are of a higher standard than most, an increasingly crucial factor in the selling of a country record in the modern age. More importantly, McEntire's own company, Starstruck, is a fully integrated corporation that handles all her affairs. Her husband is her manager and her company deals with everything from touring to the fan club. As McEntire says, 'I like to have control. If something goes wrong there's nobody to blame, but I much prefer keeping an input on all the different facets of being a recording artist.' Tragedy struck in 1991 when a charter plane carrying seven of her band members and her road manager crashed in a Californian mountainside, killing all aboard. Her next album, *From The Heart*, was sombre but

strong, and strength has been a continuing factor in McEntire's journey in country music.

Both Skaggs and McEntire were country veterans by the time they really made their mark with a back to country roots sound. The Judds, however, appeared just as the new traditionalist trend was under way and have been the top duo in country music ever since. Their stripped-down, acoustic-based music proved a welcome antidote to the production excesses of country pop and was accepted almost immediately. Mother Naomi and daughter Wynona sang at home for fun and Naomi reasoned that Wynona had such a strong voice she could make a career with it. While working as a nurse, Naomi treated record producer Brent Maher's daughter and managed to pass a home-recorded demo tape to Maher. He loved the sound and in 1984 The Judds made their début for RCA and had two number ones, 'Why Not Me' and 'Mama He's Crazy'. Since then they have rarely been out of the charts, have won countless awards and more significantly were part of the initial wave of artists who wanted to take country music back to its roots. Ill-health forced Naomi to retire from performing in 1991, though the Judd sound continues with the solo career of the big-voiced daughter Wynona.

While Skaggs and The Judds brought back the old-time mountain sound, George Strait from Texas reminded country music of the power and beauty of laid-back honky-tonk and western swing. Strait has been a commercial phenomenon and his records have rarely been out of the charts. He has consistently broken concert attendance

Above, George Strait collects the Entertainer of the Year award at the CMA awards show in 1990.

Left, The album that launched Strait in 1981.

Opposite, Mother and daughter duo, The Judds, took country music by storm in the mid 80s; but, sadly, things came to an end when mother Naomi (left) retired due to serious illness. Daughter Wynonna's solo career commenced in spectacular fashion as her debut solo album sold one million copies in six days!

Right, George Strait has continued to enjoy phenomenal and consistent success throughout the 80s and into the 90s. He is now sponsored by Budweiser.

Bottom, Like the other leading lights of Nashville, Strait has his own souvenir emporium.

Above, Queues surround the legendary Ryman Auditorium, once home of the Grand Ole Opry in downtown Nashville.

records, selling out stadium gigs in as little as twenty minutes at times. He has had over twenty number ones since his début in 1981, three gold and three platinum albums. He has also been voted one of the fifty most beautiful people in the world by *People* magazine. While others liked the idea of going back to basics in country music, Strait already had. He gained his first singing experience in the army with songs by his musical heroes Merle Haggard, Bob Wills and Hank Williams. After the army he returned to Texas, tried farming, but could not settle and instead put together the Ace In The Hole band and found bar work around Texas. Spotted by ex-MCA promotions man Erv Woolsey, Strait and the band were signed to MCA. His first single, 'Unwound', went top ten. Strait's style is old-time hard country. His voice is pure and deep, the band rough and shimmering in all the right places. Something of a Nashville outsider, Strait has tended to stand apart from the business community, preferring to reside in Texas when not on the road. And where other country artists spend a large percentage of their

Left, Randy Travis (born Randy Traywick) had a reputation as a tearaway teenager before becoming a great star of country music in the late 80s.

Below, Travis has one of the classiest gift stores in Nashville.

working time on the publicity and interview trail, Strait likes to let his records do the talking.

With signs in Nashville that a new approach was healthy, the record companies actively looked for new talent. They wanted freshness and youth tied to an older style. Every record company wanted the next big star. And in the late 80s no star shone brighter than Randy Travis. His first album, *Storms Of Life*, went gold faster than any other début release in country music history. But, as with most overnight sensations, Travis had in fact been playing music and paying those dues for many a year. From North Carolina Travis, whose real name is Randy Traywick, grew up listening to old records by country legends Ernest Tubb, Lefty Frizzell, Hank Williams and George Jones. At sixteen he won a talent contest and gained a regular spot in a club owned by his manager-to-be, Lib Hatcher. In 1981 Travis

and Hatcher headed for Nashville, convinced that Travis' voice and style were perfect for the contemporary country scene. But for three years everybody turned him down. Finally in 1985, with Nashville convinced that a back to basics approach was the future, Warners signed the plaintive-voiced Travis, achieved three number ones in a few months and saw the début album go gold. The album was a throwback to the best work of George Jones and Merle Haggard. Older fans could not believe that Travis was less than thirty, so mature and world-weary were his vocals. At the same time, younger people were drawn to his music. His follow-up album, *Always And Forever*, broke new sales records. In 1987 Travis was voted CMA male vocalist of the year. Clearly country had a new star. His thunder may have been stolen in the 90s, but Travis remains a chart-topping artist whose albums still suggest a firm belief in the value of traditional country music.

The new traditionalist or new country movement as it became known played a vital role in changing country music demographics. Suddenly, with many of the older artists taking a back seat, country music began to appeal to younger audiences. The more minimalist sound fitted easier with rock music. But it was Dwight Yoakam, the born-again honky-tonker from Kentucky, whose style and

Above, Dwight Yoakam and Buck Owens. A big fan of Owens, Yoakam finally dragged him out of retirement to play shows and to cut a few duets.

Top, Dwight Yoakam is as well known for his skin-tight jeans as for his nasal, yodelling vocals. Yoakam achieved success despite upsetting the Nashville establishment with some outspoken comments.

outspoken militancy played a major role in bringing the new style of country to a broader audience. Yoakam played old-time honky-tonk but with a rock and roll mentality. He dressed western but sexy and his barrage of attacks on the Nashville establishment excited the rock media. From Pikeville, Kentucky, he grew up with old-time country. 'Country music was all I heard, it was Hank Williams and Bill Monroe.' Yoakam chose a musical career and went to Nashville in the mid 70s. His style at that time was out of sync with mainstream Nashville. 'They said I was too country.' Dismayed and confused, Yoakam gave up on Nashville and went to the west coast. In Los Angeles he made a conscious decision to avoid the country bars where the money was good and play instead to rock audiences. His band opened for the likes of Los Lobos and The Blasters, for he was convinced that hard country had as much relevance to kids as punk and rock. 'Bill Monroe and Hank Williams were the predecessors of rock and roll,' he claimed. His plan worked and before long Warners gave Yoakam a chance. His début album *Guitars Cadillacs Etc.* made quite a stir. A strong live following ensured that the album sold well and it seemed likely that Yoakam could return to Nashville a star. Unfortunately some harsh criticisms of music city to the British rock press caused problems and, although he later backtracked, he has remained somewhat of a country music outsider. A great fan of Buck Owens, Yoakam played a key role in reviving the career of the Bakersfield legend who appeared on Yoakam's *Buenas Noches From A Lonely Room* album in 1988. That action brought Owens out of retirement and into a new record deal with Capitol.

kdLang, like Yoakam, caused some controversy in Nashville when she first appeared. As with Yoakam, Lang's attitude propelled her towards a rock environment but her musical love was country. Artistically Nashville could not ignore her stunning vocals, but her image worried some. Her short cropped haircut and sombre black outfits were hardly the normal attire for country music women. But again, as with Yoakam, her image inspired interest from outside the normal country base. Lang, from Canada, grew up singing and at an early age fell for the majesty of Loretta Lynn and Patsy Cline. By 1983 she had her own band, The Reclines, and she cut an album, *Angel With A Lariat*, with Dave Edmunds at the helm. It was rough and spiky, with Lang's vocals cutting sharp through a wall of electric noise. She was still too off the wall for Nashville. Her second album, however, caused ripples of excitement. A Patsy Cline fanatic, Lang somehow drew

Cline's producer Owen Bradley out of retirement for her monumental *Shadowlands* album. Bradley's seal of approval and the awesome sound of the album gained Lang several friends in Nashville. Lang has since moved away from country music but her Nashville albums are vocal masterpieces and her role in bringing new fans to country and challenging Nashville's view of women has been vital.

The open-door atmosphere in Nashville in the mid 80s brought a host of artists to Tennessee in search of a break. Once again Nashville was buzzing and thriving. New signings were on the rise and new styles and new ideas were in vogue. Record company executives like Jimmy

Above, kdLang (actually Kathy Dawn) comes from Canada. Nashville accepted her despite her androgynous image. She has now moved into films as well as songs.

Opposite, Nanci Griffith from Texas lies somewhere between pop, folk and country. One of the brightest new country artists, she is also a novelist and an expert on Texan culture.

Bowen and Joe Galante brought rock sales and promotion techniques to Nashville. Bowen's work guiding the careers of George Strait and Reba McEntire, and later as head of Liberty Records, has made him just as significant behind the scenes as Chet Atkins and Owen Bradley were in their day. Tony Brown, producer and A & R director at MCA, played a key role in signing some of the more idiosyncratic talent to appear at that time. Brown worked with three key artists, Lyle Lovett, Nanci Griffith and Steve Earle. All three have since moved away from Nashville, but for a while it looked as if their unique and quirky styles could fit happily into the more open-minded country music world.

Steve Earle's 1986 album, *Guitar Town*, captured the imagination of the new country market. Earle was by no means a new traditionalist. His songs were pure country, but his musical expression leaned more towards John Cougar Mellencamp. A Texan, Earle began as a folkie inspired by heroes Guy Clark and Townes Van Zandt. 'As a kid I hated country music . . . but those Outlaw guys . . . got me into it.' He survived as a songwriter for several years, made an unsuccessful neo-rockabilly album for CBS and finally hooked up with Tony Brown at MCA. *Guitar Town* was a little rocky for country radio but there was no doubting Earle's country roots and abilities. Subsequent albums saw Earle move slowly away from country music, although he has no time for musical labels. 'To me good rock and good country are very close. It's all about honesty and passion and emotion.' Earle's outspoken manner and political interests drew him to a rock crowd, but whether he can move from a Springsteen-flavoured country sound to being a fully fledged rocker remains to be seen.

Tony Brown picked up on another Texan who was just as off centre in Nashville terms as Steve Earle. Lovett's wordy,

Above, kdLang initially surprised Nashville with her uncompromising musical style and androgynous image. She went on to achieve acclaim as one of today's great country vocalists.

Right, Steve Earle brought some much-needed bite and anger back into country music with his début album *Guitar Town*. He has since confused Nashville by fusing country with heavy metal.

Opposite, Kathy Mattea, a former guide in the Country Music Hall of Fame, is now one of the most respected artists in Nashville.

Below, Kathy Mattea playing baseball in the American Sports section of the annual Fan Fair in Nashville.

Right, Vince Gill learned his craft in the bluegrass world before becoming a mainstream star and being named male vocalist of 1991 at the CMA award show.

jazzy style was far gentler than Earle's rocking band sound, but around 1984 country music was still experimenting, still looking for the new sound. Lovett, with his Eraserhead haircut and tall lanky presence, looked odd. His songs were quirky and his band was primarily a jazz band. Not easy to bracket, some of Lovett's singles were aimed at a jazz rather than a country market, but his individuality has been his greatest asset. He is a trained journalist and his songs are lyrical gems, highlighting the unusual.

Nanci Griffith, another Texan, also received her major label breakthrough thanks to Tony Brown at MCA. A friend of Lyle Lovett from Texas, Griffith was very much part of the mid 80s new wave of country music, playing a significant role in taking country into college radio and a rock market. Griffith's style, like that of her new country cohorts, was rootsy and sparse, especially in contrast to what had gone before. Griffith was playing honky-tonks at the age of fourteen. 'That was a great training ground. You don't get away with self-indulgent little love songs in places like that. It has to be direct and emotional. I learned

a lot about songwriting from playing honky-tonks as a kid.' Griffith made several albums for independent labels in Texas and never imagined that her folksy style would become part of a Nashville movement. Her début album for MCA, however, sounded pretty country, but somehow Griffith's warbly vocals did not appeal to country radio. 'They'll happily play my songs if they're sung by other people but somehow DJs don't really like my voice.' As she was not quite accepted by country radio, MCA moved her affairs to the LA office, but she has remained living and writing in rural Tennessee ever since. One of the most intelligent and challenging of contemporary country musicians, Griffith looks certain to flirt with Nashville and country for as long as she makes music.

It was Kathy Mattea who first brought Nanci Griffith's name to country music attention by recording Griffith's 'Love At The Five And Dime'. Mattea has been one of the most consistent country artists since the early 80s. She was already a recording artist before Nashville began changing and her vocals fitted perfectly into the new vein. Mattea

moved to Nashville from Virginia, worked as a tour guide at the Country Music Hall Of Fame and sang on countless demo recordings. Her début album in 1983 was not a great success but it sold well enough for her to make a follow-up. 'It was too 70s sounding, we weren't bold enough at the time to go back to basics.' Her subsequent albums have done just that, however. *Walk The Way The Wind Blows* was her breakthrough album. 'I decided to spend a lot of time preparing for that record. I realized that Nashville was again a boom town for songs, so I had to find the right material, and hunt out real quality tunes.' She had a massive across-the-board hit in 1990 with 'Where've You Been', which was co-written by her husband, John Vezner.

Another husband and wife were successful in the mid to late 80s, though separately. Vince Gill slowly established himself as a solo artist after years in the shadows while his wife Janice found great success with the sparky sister act Sweethearts Of The Rodeo. Gill fitted perfectly into the new traditionalist mood. He started out in bluegrass bands before teaming up with Rodney Crowell for his Cherry Bombs band. Gill's high harmony singing and slide guitar playing won him plenty of session work. It was his old friend Tony Brown who set him on his recording way but he could not find that magic hit ingredient. Gill slipped from attention for a while, concentrating on writing before bouncing back with his seminal third album *The Way Back Home*, a sterling pot-pourri of country styles set against a backing of delicately played acoustic instruments.

The Sweethearts Of The Rodeo appeared seemingly from nowhere in 1987. Janice and Kristine Oliver hailed from California, took their name from The Byrds' album and sang country rock on the west coast. When Janice married Vince Gill and moved to Nashville their musical ambitions were put on the back burner. Soon, however, Kristine also moved to Nashville and the duo won a Wrangler country showdown contest. And after a showcase concert CBS signed the duo. Their first album yielded five hit singles. Their punchy rocking style was typified in their early hit. As the 90s turned, the Sweethearts were placed as one of the strongest duos in country music.

The proof that the new artists really did make a difference lies in the response to the challenge from the more

Right, President Nixon gives his stamp of approval to country music by presenting Glen Campbell at the White House.

Above, The Oakridge Boys, purveyors of beautiful mountain harmonies.

Left, There is still room in country music for eclectic offerings. The Texas Tornadoes (including Flaco Jimenez, Augie Meyers, Doug Sahm and Freddie Fenderwas) play Tex-Mex country rock.

Opposite, top, K. T. Oslin appeared, apparently from nowhere, in the late 80s with sophisticated and thoughtful country music. She wrote from a woman's point of view and proved enormously successful.

established names. Artists like Barbara Mandrell and Glen Campbell who had become the epitome of country crossover started stripping down their own productions and going for a sparser, more country sound. Other younger artists like Tanya Tucker and Rosanne Cash thrived on the support and produced some of their best work in the late 1980s. Tucker, who had surfaced as a Billy Sherrill protégé in the early 70s while still a kid, burst back on the scene in 1988 with the rootsy 'Strong Enough To Bend' and won the CMA female vocalist award in 1991. In many ways Rosanne Cash predated the freewheeling attitudes of the new breed. In the late 70s she was making records, talking about drugs and writing songs with very real and relevant lyrics. Her breakthrough album *Seven-Year Ache* from 1980 contained two number ones and won a Grammy nomination. Hardly prolific, she has picked her times to put out records and two recent efforts, *Rhythm And Romance* and *King's Record Shop*, have seen her move slowly away from country to a more rock environment.

While new artists in the 80s gave Nashville a much-needed cutting edge, several more mainstream artists continued to maintain their careers. Vern Gosdin continued to make impeccable pure country records. Earl Thomas Conley from Ohio hit the number one spot in 1980 with 'Fire And Smoke' and repeated that feat another twenty times throughout the 1980s without ever selling millions of albums or getting the media attention of some of his contemporaries. Asleep At The Wheel, the best-known western swing band in country music, won Grammys in 1987 and 1988 for 'String Of Pearls' and 'Sugarfoot Rag'. Gary Morris launched his career in 1983 with the hit 'Wind Beneath My Wings' and continued to have hits throughout the 80s. Eddie Rabbitt, who grabbed national attention in the mid 70s, continued to put out excellent records and has twenty-six number one hits to his name. But the most significant change in the 80s was a move away from synthesiser-heavy formula country crossover and a return to a nostalgic update of old-time country music. Traditional country music instrumentation was in vogue and there was a host of young new acts who played music rooted in old styles but with a strong contemporary feel.

Top right, The Bellamy Brothers are country rock stalwarts, best known for the hit song 'Let Your Love Flow'.

Right, Rodney Crowell, husband of Rosanne Cash is a recording artist with several hits to his name.

Left, Paul Overstreet, leading light of the new breed of Nashville songwriters. Overstreet wrote several hits for Randy Travis and has recorded a number of albums in his own right.

Bottom, Eddie Rabbitt is still going strong after winning worldwide success in the 80s.

Below, Waylon Jennings (in cowboy hat) brought a much-needed sense of fun to country music in the 70s.

5
Country
Now

T he start of the 90s brought an unprecedented boom in country music. It was no longer the sound of the Southern rural states; wherever you went in the US, from New York to Los Angeles, you would have no trouble finding country music on the radio. In early 1991 the American business magazine *Forbes* ran a cover story on the country boom. The message was 'Rock's Out', 'Country's In'. Country's popularity has turned it into a business with a revenue of more than three billion dollars. The magazine discovered that in one week in January country accounted for twenty per cent of all records sold. When country TV host Ralph Emery wrote his autobiography it went to the top of the bestseller charts.

The cable company, The Nashville Network, is proving popular across America, not just in the South. Industry veteran Buddy Killen is quoted as saying, 'Country has just become the hottest thing. There are more gold and plati-

num records now than I remember. It just seems to be neverending. There was a time when for someone to sell half a million records was really something. Now it's becoming a common occurrence.'

This sudden revelation was brought about partly because the music industry bible, *Billboard*, changed its chart technique. Instead of taking estimates from record store owners, the magazine now uses a more accurate tabulation system that covers purchases in general stores like K Mart, where country records are more likely to be bought. Perhaps the rise is not so dramatic after all, and country sales might have been far more significant than previously thought. Other factors, however, justify the theory that country is in a boom. The growth in country radio stations has been prodigious. There are now nearly 2,500 such stations, more than for any other format. Moreover, the share value of Gaylord Entertainment Co., which owns TNN (The Nashville Network cable operation, The Grand Ole Opry, the Opryland Hotel, WSM radio and the Opryland theme park), has gone through the roof.

Whatever the sociological theories – such as the idea that country booms in times of recession since it relates directly to hard times – there is no doubt that without the charismatic appeal and phenomenal success of one man the rise may not have been so dramatic and certainly not so fast. That artist is Garth Brooks, possibly the most amazing success story in country music history. Garth Brooks is currently the most successful male artist in country and with three albums in the top five of the *Billboard* album chart he is also the most popular artist in all forms of music. Brooks arrived in Nashville in 1987. It was his second attempt to carve a career for himself. In three months he had a record deal and was in the studio with Allen Reynolds, the man who had pointed the musical way for both Crystal Gayle and Kathy Mattea. His début album produced four major hits. The second album, *No Fences*, was even more successful and his third album, *Ropin' The Wind*, spent over three months at the top of the main album charts and became the most successful country record ever.

Brooks' success lies very much in his groundbreaking live shows. Where country performers have typically stood and sung their songs, Brooks has taken on the highly professional stage visuals of a top-notch rock show. Guitars are occasionally smashed, lights flash and Brooks works himself into a frenzy on stage. Country music has seen nothing like it and the fans have responded by making Brooks America's most popular entertainer in 1991.

But while Brooks surfaced with an eclectic style and a

Previous page, centre, Garth Brooks entered the 90s as the artist who was destined to shake up not only the country music world but also the pop music industry with the biggest selling album of all time, *Ropin' The Wind*.

Previous page, top, Trisha Yearwood burst onto the Nashville scene with a début single that topped the charts, the first time this had happened in twenty-five years.

Above, Another significant milestone in Garth Brooks' career was October 6, 1990, when he was made a member of the Grand Ole Opry. Announcing the induction was singer-songwriter, Johnny Russell, whose many hits include "Act Naturally".

Left, Multi-award winner Garth Brooks swept the board at the 1991 Academy of Country Music Awards, when he won in all six categories in which he was nominated, including the prestigious Entertainer of the Year.

Below, A Garth Brooks fan, an early promotional item which gave no indication of the heat that he was later to create!

Above, Clint Black and Roy Rogers at the 1991 CMA awards show. The two have become firm friends, although Roy Rogers, who has always played the good guy, has been careful to keep the white hat.

new approach, he was by no means alone in setting new musical standards. Before Brooks' dramatic rise it appeared that a honky-tonk singer, Clint Black, was set to be the new King Of Country. Black's style is slightly more traditional than that of Brooks, but he too softened the country sound with some singer-songwriter meanderings. His first single went to number one and both his albums, *Killin' Time* and *Put Yourself In My Shoes*, have gone platinum.

Alan Jackson has also given Brooks a close run in the popularity stakes in the early 90s. Jackson, from Newman, Georgia, has had a meteoric rise. His first album, *Here In The Real World*, went gold and his second, *Don't Rock The Jukebox*, platinum. In 1991 he was nominated for a string of awards. Like Brooks and Black, Jackson is a songwriter and writes or co-writes most of the songs he records. George

Top left, Clint Black, leading member of the hat acts, found success partly thanks to clever management by Bill Ham (ZZ Top manager). He is married to television star, Lisa Hartman.

Above, Clint Black gets to perform on the same bill as pig races.

Left, Alan Jackson from Georgia would surely have won an armful of awards had he not surfaced at the same time as Garth Brooks.

Right, The easy flowing group Shenandoah have kept the sweet sound of high harmony alive in modern country music.

Below, Highway 101 gave country an edge in the 80s. Lead singer, Paulette Carlson, has since left the band for a solo career.

Jones was clearly a great influence on Jackson's music. Jones performed a duet with Jackson on 'Just Playin' Possum' and appeared in the video for 'Don't Rock The Jukebox'.

The 80s and 90s have also seen a growth in popularity for country groups. In the late 80s Shenandoah and Restless Heart burst on to the scene with a very accomplished soft country rock sound. Shenandoah came out of a Muscle Shoals band MSM before turning to slick country with hits like 'Mama Knows' and 'Two Dozen Roses'. The band went through a lull in their career during some legal difficulties over their name, but 1992 sees the band clear to go back to the charts. Restless Heart, the concept of producer Tim Dubois, now head of Arista Records, consists of five

Above, Restless Heart rival Shenandoah and Sawyer Brown for recognition as the top country group.

Right, A little rougher than Restless Heart and Shenandoah, Sawyer Brown have scored several big hits, and look as though they may achieve superstar status.

excellent musicians whose harmony-laden sound has won them several hit singles and heavy album sales, recalling the easy sound of The Eagles at their best.

Highway 101 also appeared in the late 80s. More rocky than Shenandoah or Restless Heart, they quickly made their name with pure country with a rock beat. They won the CMA best group award in 1988 and looked set to sell millions of records for many years. However, lead singer Paulette Carlson opted for a solo career, and while her fortunes are yet to be determined, the band, with new singer Niki Nelson, continue to have hits. Another group, Sawyer Brown, have been around for some time. They won the CMA's Horizon award in 1985 after winning a talent contest the year before and have enjoyed a string of hits.

Above, Steve Wariner, Ricky Skaggs, Mark O'Connor and Vince Gill collecting instrumental awards at the 1991 CMA awards.

Below, Patty Loveless has matured dramatically since her début in the mid 80s and is currently one of the most popular and respected singers in Nashville.

Right, Ricky Van Shelton, another hat act, has sold consistently well since the late 80s.

The 90s have been good for several artists who first appeared in the wake of the new country boom. Ricky van Shelton, a rocker turned country singer, paid his dues for years before surfacing in Nashville in 1987. Shelton has locked his style into the honky-tonk sound of Jones, Haggard and Tubb. His début album, *Wild-Eyed Dream*, gave him three straight number ones and he picked up numerous awards in 1988 and 1989. Van Shelton may have been lost temporarily in the wake of Garth Brooks and Clint Black, but his 1991 album, *Backroads*, is selling as well as previous offerings. Steve Wariner has been on the scene for many a year but has peaked in the 90s. He began his career in the late 70s, was a protégé of Chet Atkins and made several pop country releases. A more country sound in the late 80s has revitalized his career and he is regarded as one of the top guitarists in Nashville.

Patty Loveless first made her mark in the 80s with some perfectly crafted new traditionalist but progressive-minded records. From Pikeville, Kentucky, from where Dwight Yoalkam also came, she first went to Nashville as a fourteen-year-old girl and got herself an audition with

Porter Wagobener. For several years she sang with the Wilburns. Marriage, however, pushed her away from singing but she came back to the fold just as country music opened its doors to fresh talent and new ideas. Since the 80s she has consolidated her position with hits like 'Lonely Side Of Life' and 'Timber, I'm Falling In Love'.

And should any of the top sellers produce a weak record, there are countless new names waiting to step into their shoes. Joe Diffie, a top session singer, had enormous success with his first Epic Records album. His début single, 'Home', went to number one and he continues to rack up the hits. Hal Ketchum from Texas sounds less mainstream than many others, but Nashville has taken to his literary songs and powerful delivery. Pam Tillis, daughter of Mel, had worked in the backrooms of Nashville for years mainly as a writer before setting out on a solo career. Her self-titled album quickly gave her a number one hit and Tillis looks set to be a major country star over the next few years. Trisha Yearwood had a more dramatic rise to the top than others. She worked as a record company receptionist and sang demos for a while, befriending Garth Brooks. When Brooks made it big he rewarded the friendship with a slot on his tour. Yearwood was made and her first single went to number one.

Below, Singer-songwriter, Hal Ketchum from Texas, is proving popular among rock as well as country audiences with his thoughtful songs and powerful singing.

Left, Joe Diffie is a recent arrival clearly destined for big things with a mixture of down home tear-jerkers and snappy rock numbers.

Next page, top, Keith Whitley struggled for a long time before finally making it big in the late 80s. His untimely death from alcohol poisoning ended a promising career.

Next page, bottom, Keith Whitley and his wife Lorrie Morgan signing autographs at Fan Fair. Since Keith's death, Morgan has immersed herself in her own career and proved to be a major star.

Opposite, top, The Kentucky Headhunters brought some welcome irreverence to Nashville with their outstanding début, 'Electric Barnyard'. They even had a hit with a cover of 'The Ballad of Davy Crockett'.

Opposite, bottom, Mark O'Connor is the top fiddle player on the session scene in Nashville. He is also a gifted guitarist, and has made several solo albums for the Masters series on MCA.

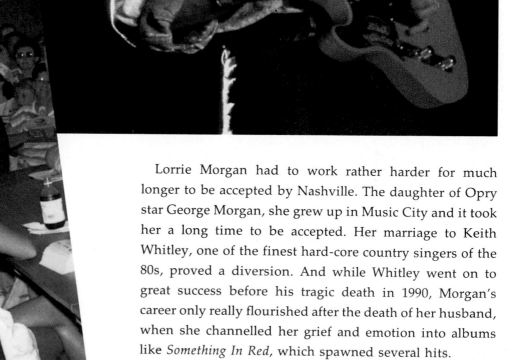

Lorrie Morgan had to work rather harder for much longer to be accepted by Nashville. The daughter of Opry star George Morgan, she grew up in Music City and it took her a long time to be accepted. Her marriage to Keith Whitley, one of the finest hard-core country singers of the 80s, proved a diversion. And while Whitley went on to great success before his tragic death in 1990, Morgan's career only really flourished after the death of her husband, when she channelled her grief and emotion into albums like *Something In Red*, which spawned several hits.

The Kentucky Headhunters were the most successful country group of 1990 and 1991. Much tougher in sound than Restless Heart and Sawyer Brown, the Headhunters play southern rock laced with pure country. The band are popular with heavy metal fans as well as with country aficionados and have surprised many in Nashville. They

even got away with a version of 'Ballad Of Davy Crockett' and its accompanying off-the-wall video. The Headhunters have brought a touch of humour and zest into Nashville and were rewarded when their début album *Pickin' On Nashville* went gold faster than any other début album by a group in the history of country music. In 1991 they reportedly played some of the wildest shows in country music supporting Hank Williams Jr.

The upsurge in interest in country music has led to record companies signing more and more new artists. And while some slip by the wayside, as has always happened, the growing exposure is producing potential new stars by the month. Doug Stone has set the charts alight since his début 'I'd Be Better Off In A Pine Box' from his first album,

Doug Stone, on Epic. Like Alan Jackson, he hails from Newman, Georgia, and first appeared on stage as a child opening a show near Atlanta for Loretta Lynn. Mark Chesnutt has enjoyed a successful start to the 90s. His music is close to that of George Strait, he too comes from Texas and his début album *Too Cold At Home* is the biggest-selling début album in MCA Nashville's long history. Lionel Cartwright, a Tony Brown protégé, is bubbling under with three albums for MCA and Suzy Bogguss, who has been on the fringes for a while, looks set to take on all comers with her broad country sound.

With all these new artists proving successful and breaking sales and attendance records, country music really is in its most exciting and solid state ever. Older, more estab-

lished artists still have their role to play and the interest in country across America has never been equalled. The cable operation The Nashville Network reaches into around twenty-eight million homes across America, and the country music radio audience is now bigger than that for Top 40 and album rock.

Nashville itself still attracts a host of tourists all year round. The various museums and gift stores provide not just souvenirs but a picture of country music history. The Opry and the Opryland complex continue to expand dramatically. The shows at the Opry's Ryman auditorium were so popular that in the early 70s the Opry had to move home. In 1974 the Grand Ole Opry was relocated in a 400 acre-Opryland complex which also houses a theme park,

Opposite, Mary Chapin Carpenter is another singer who can hardly be described as a purely country musician. She stole the show at the 1991 CMA awards with a performance of rare vitality and abandon (top).

Above, Fiddling Championship at the annual Fan Fair in Nashville.

Next page, top, The fans see a mass of stars as the Mercury Records show climaxes at the 1986 Fan Fair. Tom T. Hall, Jerry Lee Lewis, Kathy Mattea, Carl Parkins, Donna Fargo, The Maines Brothers, Johnny Paycheck and Lynn Anderson are among the artists on stage.

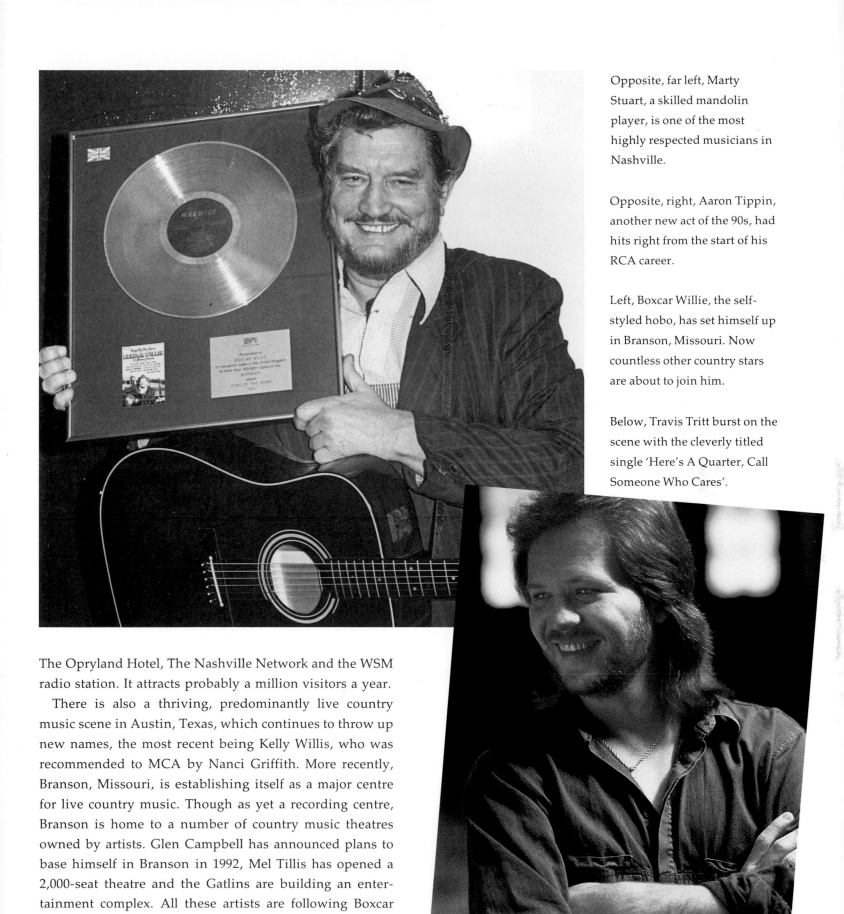

Opposite, far left, Marty Stuart, a skilled mandolin player, is one of the most highly respected musicians in Nashville.

Opposite, right, Aaron Tippin, another new act of the 90s, had hits right from the start of his RCA career.

Left, Boxcar Willie, the self-styled hobo, has set himself up in Branson, Missouri. Now countless other country stars are about to join him.

Below, Travis Tritt burst on the scene with the cleverly titled single 'Here's A Quarter, Call Someone Who Cares'.

The Opryland Hotel, The Nashville Network and the WSM radio station. It attracts probably a million visitors a year.

There is also a thriving, predominantly live country music scene in Austin, Texas, which continues to throw up new names, the most recent being Kelly Willis, who was recommended to MCA by Nanci Griffith. More recently, Branson, Missouri, is establishing itself as a major centre for live country music. Though as yet a recording centre, Branson is home to a number of country music theatres owned by artists. Glen Campbell has announced plans to base himself in Branson in 1992, Mel Tillis has opened a 2,000-seat theatre and the Gatlins are building an entertainment complex. All these artists are following Boxcar Willie, who first made Branson his musical home.

Country music is in its strongest position ever, the sound is diverse, new artists are constantly arising alongside established names and the Nashville industry is challenging the historical dominance of pop and rock music in the United States.

Index

Acknowledgements

Many thanks to George Strait, together with his manager, Erv Woolsey, and P.R. lady Kay West, for providing the foreword.

Much appreciation is also due to the various Nashville record companies, managements and agencies, all too numerous to mention (but certainly not forgotten), for supplying information and photographs on their respective artists.

Finally, a debt of gratitude (for their great assistance) to the Country Music Association; the Grand Ole Opry and the Opryland organisation; the Chamber of Commerce/Tourist Boards of Fort Worth, Nashville and Tennessee; and Byworth-Wootton, country music's home office in London!

Other photo credits as listed:
Academy of Country Music: 101, 129; *Donnie Beauchamp:* 128; *Robert Blakeman:* 93; *Adrian Boot: Tony Byworth:* 42 (bottom); 99 (bottom), 114 (bottom), 115 (bottom); *James Colburn:* 58 (top); *Jacqueline A. Dagnall:* 79, 84 (top); *Kelly Delaney:* 57; *Fort Worth Chamber Of Commerce:* 24, 102, 131 (bottom); *Kathy Gangwisch:* 125 (bottom); *Steve Goldstein:* 40 (top); *Greg Gorman:* 89 (top left); *Beth Gwinn:* 86, 94 (bottom), 107 (bottom), 110 (bottom), 113 (top), 120 (left), 130 (and back jacket), 131 (bottom), 138 (top); *George Hamilton IV Collection:* 51; *Grand Ole Opry/Opryland:* 18, 27 (bottom), 34; *Ron Keith:* 135 (bottom); *Les Leverett:* 54 (top); *Terry Lott:* 87 (bottom); *Alan L. Mayor:* 28, 48 (bottom), 78, 80, 87 (top), 116 (bottom), 134 (top), 135 (top), 136 (bottom), 140 (top); *McGuire:* 110 (top), 120 (centre), 124 (bottom), 127; *Chaim Mekel:* 133 (bottom); *Alan Messer:* 63 (bottom), 82 (top), 90, 140 (left); *Peter Nash:* 137 (both), 141 (both); *Nashville Chamber Of Commerce:* 45 (top), 46, 47; *Peter Newark's Western Americana:* 8, 9, 10 (both), 11, 12, 13 (bottom), 17, 25; *Frank Okenfels:* 133 (top); *Beverley Parker:* 126, 129 (and front jacket); *Buddy Rosenberg:* 85; *Randee St. Nicholas:* 134 (bottom); *Carl Saunders:* 141 (top); *Norman Seeff:* 62; *Tennessee Tourist Office:* 97; *Bill Van Overback:* 123 (bottom); *Kitty Wells Collection:* 39; *C. Williams:* 52 (bottom).